It's the Law!

A practical guide to how the law affects you

Austin Lafferty, Solicitor

LexisNexis™ UK

Members of the LexisNexis Group worldwide

United Kingdom	LexisNexis UK, a Division of Reed Elsevier (UK) Ltd, 4 Hill Street, EDINBURGH EH2 3JZ and Halsbury House, 35 Chancery Lane, LONDON WC2A 1EL
Argentina	LexisNexis Argentina, BUENOS AIRES
Australia	LexisNexis Butterworths, CHATSWOOD, New South Wales
Austria	LexisNexis Verlag ARD Orac GmbH & Co KG, VIENNA
Canada	LexisNexis Butterworths, MARKHAM, Ontario
Chile	LexisNexis Chile Ltda, SANTIAGO DE CHILE
Czech Republic	Nakladatelství Orac sro, PRAGUE
France	Editions du Juris-Classeur SA, PARIS
Germany	LexisNexis Deutschland GmbH, FRANKFURT, MUNSTER
Hong Kong	LexisNexis Butterworths, HONG KONG
Hungary	HVG-Orac, BUDAPEST
India	LexisNexis Butterworths, NEW DELHI
Ireland	LexisNexis, DUBLIN
Italy	Giuffrè Editore, MILAN
Malaysia	Malayan Law Journal Sdn Bhd, KUALA LUMPUR
New Zealand	LexisNexis Butterworths, WELLINGTON
Poland	Wydawnictwo Prawnicze LexisNexis, WARSAW
Singapore	LexisNexis Butterworths, SINGAPORE
South Africa	LexisNexis Butterworths, DURBAN
Switzerland	Stämpfli Verlag AG, BERNE
USA	LexisNexis, DAYTON, Ohio

© Reed Elsevier (UK) Ltd 2004

Published by LexisNexis UK

A CIP Catalogue record for this book is available from the British Library.

ISBN 0 406 96988 4

Typeset by LexisNexis UK

Printed by Thomson Litho Ltd, East Kilbride, Scotland

Visit LexisNexis UK at www.lexisnexis.co.uk

Judge Tedd

Bear-faced Justice

Preface

The basics of civilised law are easily enough understood: no stealing, no violence and no false witness. Indeed, the ten commandments are a rough and ready legal system in themselves and still reflect our social cornerstones. Modern law has had to become more complex to deal with new situations and technology, for instance: what are the legal requirements to prove a debt; what is the status of an electronic promise or how much cooling-off time must an online finance company allow you when selling you credit? Your answers to all these and more questions may be the same: 'I don't know, but I can ask a lawyer to advise me'.

What happens if you have already committed an offence or incurred a liability, and find yourself being prosecuted or sued? The answer may come too late to help you, so just as in medicine, prevention is often better than cure.

There is little public provision for most of us to know the law. In Scotland, we have a special legal rule: 'ignorance of the law is no excuse'. This seems illogical: after all, how can you break a law if you don't know it's there? How can you be guilty of a crime if you don't know you were committing one? This is, however, how our legal system has operated for centuries. *It's the Law!* tries to give some general legal guidance to readers.

It would be more than a lifetime's work to know all our law, let alone write it down. In addition, the law rarely stands still for long. You won't expect to be a lawyer after dipping into these pages, but you should be able to find a way forward, to decide if you need professional legal help, or to get a better understanding of what a lawyer has already said.

I have concentrated on the most popular, if that's the right word, problems and questions of law that face the Scottish citizen. At the end of the book there is also a list of useful names, offices, addresses, phone and fax numbers, websites and email addresses for readers to consult further. My own firm's address, telephone, website and email locations are at the back of the book, so feel free to let me know if this book has been helpful.

I would like to thank my researchers Laura Maguire and Roger Mackenzie for their work in organising many of the FAQs and collating the list of helpful addresses. Thanks are also due to the editorial, production and marketing departments of LexisNexis UK and particularly to Jenny Blair for thinking up the project and encouraging and supporting me in its development, and finally to all those colleagues who have read the book as a draft and given advice or made comments. Any errors, however, remain mine.

Austin Lafferty

April 2004

Contents

x

Chapter 1

Marriage and Family Law

CHORES
DO DISHES
MOW CAT
HOOVER
HEDGE
IRON
GOLDFISH

JUDGY LIQUID

A LAFFERTY

Who can and cannot get married?

As a lawyer I am mainly involved in the ending of marriages rather than
the beginning, but it is well to remember that marriage is a legal union,
and not a universal entitlement. Here are the highlights. Spouses must:

* be of different sexes;

* be outwith the forbidden degrees (this means that you cannot
  marry someone too close to you by blood, such as a parent/
  grandparent, your own child/grandchild, sibling, aunt/uncle or
  nephew/niece); and

* not be close by affinity (for example, you cannot marry your son's
  wife/daughter's husband, your own former spouse's parent or
  child).

There is a curious exception to this: you can marry, say, your deceased
wife's mother, but only if you are over 21 years old and the former wife
and her father are both dead. You cannot marry your adoptive parent or
child. You cannot be married to two persons simultaneously; this is both
the crime of bigamy and also makes the second marriage void in civil law.

It is said that the penalty for bigamy is having two mothers-in-law. Only those who genuinely consent and wish to be wed are legally married. If one spouse is forced into marriage; or did not know he or she was going through a marriage ceremony (say because of language barriers); or was too drunk to understand what was going on; or was in error as to the identity of the other party; then he or she can have the marriage annulled. If one party turns out to be incurably impotent, the marriage can also be voided if the other partner seeks a court order for nullity.

What are the legal rights and duties of husband and wife?

Love, honour and obey is the traditional answer, but real life is often more complicated. The married relationship is a web of mutual obligations. Some are positively to do things, such as to give emotional support, to love and to contribute to domestic and financial welfare. Some are negative, that is not to do things, such as not to be unfaithful, not to leave the other, not to assault or abuse. If one spouse fails, in that one or more of these duties are not done, this can lead to the marriage breaking down, and gives the other spouse the right to terminate the marriage by divorce. Obviously divorce is the ultimate sanction, and all marriages have ups and downs without having to end, but, if it comes to court, the sheriff will find out if one partner broke the rules of marriage. If so, then regret and remorse will not prevent a divorce being granted to the wronged spouse.

Is marriage a contract?

Marriage is a contract, and much more. Like a commercial agreement it imposes legal rights and duties on both participants. However, unlike a financial deal, the parties once joined cannot simply end it by agreement. Marriage changes legal status, and only a court can divide a couple up again by divorce. Even if separated for years, spouses usually retain a claim on each other's assets or even their estate on death, and cannot of course marry anyone else in the meantime. Till death, or the courts, do us part.

What is common law marriage?

Technically, this is called irregular marriage. In Scotland it has traditionally been possible to be legally married but without having gone through a wedding ceremony. There used to be three bases of such informal marriage, but now there is just one. If a couple have lived together – the legal phrase is at bed and board, so you get the picture – for a substantial period of time (the shortest time allowed by court so far is 10 months and 23 days) and if they are free to marry, that is not married to other persons and simply separated, and hold themselves out to the world as man and wife, then they may be legally married. This is not so important if things are going well for them, but if they break up, or one dies, then it may be crucial for the other to have the marriage recognised. A claim for a share of matrimonial property, or succession to the estate of a deceased spouse, will depend on the married status being established. This is done by getting a declarator of marriage from the Court of Session. Once declared by the court, the marriage can be registered like a regular one. But watch out: just living with a partner does not automatically bring about marriage. Cohabitation can be just that – living together – and if the parties do not qualify for irregular marriage, they do not have claims on each other's property.

Who has the last word in important matters?

Both spouses have equal rights in decision making.

Does the husband have to keep a roof over the heads of his wife and children? Does the husband have to maintain the wife?

The law does not use words to the effect of keeping a roof over anyone's head. If either spouse has a financial need, he or she can claim, and sue for, such maintenance or 'aliment' (not 'alimony', which is the American term) as is necessary to support him or her for a reasonable time; until the end of the marriage; or a change of circumstances. Usually maintenance between husband and wife lasts no longer than three years after either separation or divorce, though child support continues longer (see questions on child support in chapter 3).

What if my husband leaves home and doesn't give me any money?

You are entitled to pursue him at the sheriff court for aliment and, if it is urgent, for interim aliment. The test for interim aliment is your immediate financial need. If he is working, he will normally be made to pay. The decree for the maintenance can be enforced by arrestment, that is freezing of his earnings, bank accounts, or other assets so he cannot get at them or use them until the other spouse or the court allows it, usually after payment of all sums due. Legal aid is available to help you take your case to court and there is no clawback by the Scottish Legal Aid Board for recovered aliment. A hearing can be arranged at court at very short notice. Capital matters, such as a house, bank accounts, shares, insurance and pensions, all take longer to sort out. Note that, as in all matrimonial legal matters, the same is true in reverse, that is, if the wife is the earner or the main earner and leaves without giving the husband any money.

Does a husband/father have to maintain the children?

The children's right to aliment or support is from both parents; there is no order of preference. The duty to maintain is shared between the parents according to their own circumstances. Where parents have split up, the absent parent must help to maintain the children financially if he or she is earning enough. Maintenance can be agreed on or negotiated by the spouses between themselves, via their solicitors or via the Child Support Agency, which is the primary enforcement body for child maintenance. In some limited circumstances one parent can ignore the Child Support Agency and take the other to the sheriff court for aliment of children, and older children can sometimes take a parent to court too. If aliment is no longer contentious, solicitors can draw up a minute of agreement (a written contract) to regulate the amount, the frequency and the method of payments. This is signed by the parents before witnesses, and usually registered in the Books of Council and Session. It is enforceable like a court order so that if a parent fails to pay due maintenance they can have their wages and bank account arrested.

Does it matter who is to blame for the break-up of a marriage?

The 'guilty' party (as he or she used to be called) is not financially penalised for committing adultery or unreasonable behaviour. It does not matter who either caused the break-up of the marriage or left the matrimonial home, though certain misconduct will allow the other 'innocent' party to raise a divorce action. But read on . . .

Are financial settlements or awards dependent on who caused the break-up?

No. A spouse can run off with another person, be violent or desert the other spouse and still be entitled to a full fair share of the matrimonial property.

Do you have to get divorced in the country you got married in?

No. If you are domiciled or permanently resident in Scotland, it doesn't matter where you got married. Not only does the law recognise your marriage, any divorce is governed by the law of Scotland.

What are the grounds of divorce?

In law there is now only a single ground of divorce called 'irretrievable breakdown of marriage'. In fact that ground is broken down into individual causes, which are: insanity; desertion (leaving for two years); separation for two years with consent; separation for five years (no consent required); adultery (sexual intercourse with another person outwith the marriage); and unreasonable behaviour (which can include a huge range of conduct including violence, financial waste, lack of communication, withholding of sex, selfishness, drunkenness and many, many other examples). Note that marriage can also be *annulled* on special grounds, including non-consummation, deception or where someone was forced into the marriage.

What is a quickie divorce?

A divorce can be concluded without involving lawyers in a minimum of two years (remembering that among the grounds of divorce there are two *separation* causes). If the spouses have been apart for two years and both agree to divorce, or if they have been separated for five years when consent becomes irrelevant, then they can use the Simplified Procedure. However, this is only if there are no children under 16 years of age and no unresolved financial issues. If neither of those situations applies then either spouse can get the form SP2 (two years) or SP5 (five years) from the local sheriff court or the Scottish Courts website. The form is filled in, signed, notarised by a Notary Public or a solicitor, and submitted to the court with a booking fee and the marriage certificate. As long as everything is in order, the court will grant the divorce within a few weeks. There are no court hearings and there is no need for legal fees. However, if the other spouse objects, or states that they have a financial claim, the court will allow them to argue their case and not automatically grant the divorce.

What is the date of separation?

The most obvious definition of this is when the couple actually start to live in different accommodation. This does not need to be declared to lawyers or marked officially in any way by a court order or formal document, but the legal clock starts ticking when actual separation takes place. Note that you can live separately in the same house, if you are no longer living as man and wife, and are just inhabiting the same accommodation out of necessity, such as childcare, or financial limitation. The date of separation will have been when this situation first became established.

Why is the date of separation so important in divorce?

The date of separation is absolutely crucial and fundamental to spouses' rights and financial claims. The law calls the date of separation the 'relevant date' and it is used for the division of matrimonial assets between the spouses. That is the date at which life policies, bank accounts, shares and all items on which the spouses have a claim are valued (though houses in joint names may be excepted, and valued later). Even if the divorce is granted, or a settlement negotiated months or years later, and the circumstances of one or both spouses have changed drastically, it is still the date of separation that is the trigger for valuation and calculation. It comes to this: if your spouse leaves you, and next day you buy a lottery ticket and win £3 million, it belongs to you alone. If you bought it before separation, it must be shared. Note also that if you are divorcing on the grounds of two or five years' separation, it needs to be calculated from the actual separation date.

Are financial settlements affected by who leaves the house? Must I stay in the house to protect my position or financial rights?

The answer to both questions is no. A spouse who leaves the matrimonial home because of marital disharmony retains his or her full rights in the house and assets. However, if he or she fails to contribute to the house maintenance or mortgage after leaving, they may have to take a lesser share to compensate the other spouse for those expenses since they left.

Can my spouse sell the house over my head?

Not without a court order or your agreement. If the house is in joint names, then both parties need to agree before it can be sold. If it is in the name of one spouse, then the other still has automatic legal occupancy rights and cannot be made to agree to a sale except as part of an overall settlement, or by court order at the end of a divorce action that deals with all other financial items. If any two people who own property, married or not, do not both agree to a sale, then the one who does want to sell can sue the other, seeking a court order of Division and Sale. The effect of this is that the sale takes place and the proceeds are split between the parties depending on what each is entitled to. The court may refuse or delay the sale happening (even for years) if there are good reasons to do so: for example, if the home is the abode of a spouse and young children who have no alternative accommodation, or the party wanting to sell has not made a reasonable offer to the other to buy them out.

What property or assets are divided between the spouses?

Everything that is 'matrimonial property' is divided. This is a technical legal term, and includes all things (money, policies, pensions, shares, bank accounts, physical items, etc) that have accrued between the date of marriage and date of separation, whether in the wife's name, the husband's name or in joint names, anything bought for the joint use of the spouses, and a home bought as a family (but not necessarily as a matrimonial) home. Excluded are gifts from third parties, bequests, assets owned separately before marriage and assets gained after separation (see the next question for more detail). There may be special circumstances that make it fair to split money or property other than 50–50. Special circumstances are very varied. For example, where a wife is left with young children to care for and no opportunity to get higher paid employment, she may get more than 50% of the matrimonial property as she has an economic disadvantage. Another example is where one spouse contributed the proceeds of sale of a property that they owned solely before the marriage when the couple bought a house together. The contributing spouse may be entitled to recoup that value when they separate.

What is excluded from matrimonial property?

Gifts from outside the marriage belong solely to the recipient, but gifts between spouses are matrimonial property. Note that engagement or wedding gifts to the couple belong to them equally, and cannot be claimed back from the family or side of the family that gave them. Inheritances received by a spouse are not shared with the other spouse. Anything obtained after the date of separation is also excluded. If a husband leaves a wife and is then made redundant from work the following day, the wife has no claim on the redundancy payment. Children's property is also excluded.

Do I have a claim on my spouse's pension even though it is in their name alone?

Yes, though if he or she started the pension before your marriage, your claim is only against that proportion of it that amounts to the increase in its value from the date of marriage to the date of separation. This must be calculated accurately. Your claim may be for half of that increase, or a different figure, depending on various factors. If you have a lesser earning capacity than the other spouse, or are left with the care of young children, especially if a child is disabled or has special needs (indeed you may get more if you have a disability), or have some other serious financial hardship then you may get more than a 50% share. If the pension started after marriage, then you get a share of the increase from the pension start date (as that was during the marriage) to the relevant date: the date of separation.

How do I get the share of the pension I am entitled to?

There are various ways to do this now: one is to get a cash payment that represents your fair share of the pension. This can sometimes be asked for or ordered by the court, even though the pension-holding spouse cannot access the money until retirement. You can also get a pension split or a pension share so that part of the pension is transferred to you now and available to you when you reach the age of retirement or maturity. Pension actuaries are involved in making the complex calculations to bring out the transfer value of the pension.

What happens to matrimonial debts?

Matrimonial debts can be in joint names or sole names. If the expenditure was made for the purposes of the family or home, then it is shared fairly (usually equally). This includes mortgages, bank loans, overdrafts, credit cards, catalogue debts and so on. Debts resulting from gambling or selfish expenditure may be excluded from matrimonial calculation and accrue solely to the partner who incurred them.

Am I liable for my spouse's debts if they are not in our joint names?

No bank or finance company can sue you for payment of a debt that is not in your name. However, where a relationship breaks down, one spouse can have the other held responsible for a share of debt not in his or her name if it was incurred for matrimonial purposes. It will not make a connection between you and the finance company, but it may be set off against other assets or debts in your name to reach a fair balancing calculation.

How is the division of the house, assets and money actually done?

If spouses agree to negotiate financial matters, then their solicitors get receipts, statements, valuations (vouching) of the matrimonial property and debts, as at the date of separation, which is the legal trigger date for most calculations, then work out the best way of dividing everything up. Assets can be transferred from one spouse to another, from joint names to a sole name, or divided and split between the two to achieve a fair division of property. If agreement cannot be reached, or one spouse won't negotiate at all, then the only alternative is to go to court where a sheriff will impose an arrangement by court order that can be enforced. The law is the same either way, for settlement or court action, but a negotiated deal is likely to be quicker and much less expensive than a court case.

Do I need to be divorced before I can get a financial settlement?

Certainly not. Most couples negotiate an agreement for division of assets and debts out of court and well before divorce is applied for. It can be done as part of a divorce court action, but is likely to be much more expensive and take longer that way, and, unless agreement is made, it will be up to the sheriff to impose a settlement on both parties, which may suit neither. The usual and best way to proceed is for spouses to get their solicitors to negotiate on their behalf, to compare information and documentation and agree a deal. That deal is drawn up in a contract known as a minute of agreement, which can deal with capital assets, debts, maintenance and even childcare and contact. The agreement is legally binding and, once signed, cannot be undone.

What is the cost of getting a settlement?

Every case is different. Generally the more there is to argue about, and the more arguing there is, the more expensive it will be. Lawyers' fees can range from hundreds of pounds to many thousands. Legal aid (Advice and Assistance) may be available, but if you achieve a settlement, the Scottish Legal Aid Board has the right to clawback your fees from the settlement funds in certain conditions. Normally each side pays for their own costs for the preparation and completion of the minute of agreement.

What if I change my mind after the settlement is completed?

As stated above, the minute of agreement is binding. It is in full and final settlement. There are limited rights to have the agreement overturned if it is manifestly unfair, though if you had a lawyer advising you on it then it is a much more difficult task to show that you were the victim of gross unfairness. If your solicitor has failed to advise you properly, then your right of action for compensation is against him or her, rather than resulting in an ability to change the agreement.

How does the law protect a spouse from matrimonial violence or abuse?

See chapter 4.

Chapter 2

Living Together and Separation

Do I have a claim on my partner's money or property if we are not married?

Not directly. If property is not in your name or joint names, you have no claim. However, if you contributed over time to the increase in value of a partner's property, you may have a financial claim for the unjustified enrichment enjoyed by the partner. This area of law may be in the process of changing. In 2003 the Scottish Parliament looked at the concept of civil partnerships between unmarried couples (of opposite or same sex) which would give legal protections similar to some married rights; however, no new law was made at that time.

Do both unmarried parents have equal rights to children?

At the time of writing, an unmarried father has no automatic direct legal rights to his children. If he wants to get parental rights, contact (formerly known as access), or residence (formerly known as custody), then he can raise a court action to seek an order for these. He will have to show that it would be in the best interests of the child; a genetic connection to a child is not enough. However, the Scottish Parliament is considering making parental rights automatic if both parents jointly register the birth.

Does one partner have to support or maintain the other?

No. We do not, as yet, have any right of support between partners, or 'palimony' as the Americans call it.

Can one partner be liable for the other's debts?

Not without the prior agreement of both partners.

How does the law deal with same-sex relationships?

This area of law may be in the process of changing; however, currently no law covers same-sex relationships. At the moment, on break-up or death, neither partner has any financial claim on the other, and there are no rights to the pension benefits of the other, nor to any maintenance claim. Many people see this as unfair, and believe the law should develop to recognise the different ways that people choose to live their lives. Commitment to another person would then bring about not just a bond of love, but a legal one with financial consequences. Until such a law is passed, however, the married state is the only one that creates such a legal and financial bond.

How does the law deal with domestic violence in an unmarried partnership?

See chapter 4.

Chapter 3

Children

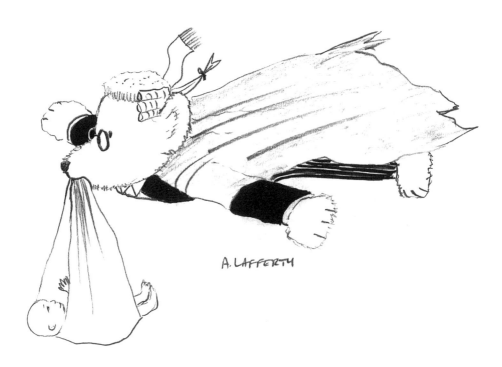

A. LAFFERTY

How much authority do parents have over children?

Parents legally have rights of residence and care of their own children up to the age of 16 years of age. It is difficult to list all the many rights that parents have. They can decide the education, health and development needs and provisions for a child, but all authority is limited by law. For example, if a parent beats a child this can be the criminal offence of assault. If the parent keeps the child off school this may be a criminal offence as parents are subject to education laws requiring them to present children for school.

Are parents responsible for their children's actions or debts?

Mainly no. There may be an exceptional situation of a parent egging a child on to commit a theft or hit another child, in which case there may be liability. Otherwise the child alone is responsible for his or her actions, although very young children may escape blame if they did not know what they were doing. At the time of writing the Scottish Parliament is talking of making parents pay for damage caused by their errant children, but nothing has yet come to pass on this. Anyone foolish enough to lend money to a child has no right to get repayment from the child's parents.

Are parents allowed to smack children?

At the moment parents can inflict reasonable (physical) chastisement on their children, though they will usually have to justify it according to the circumstances in which it is inflicted; there is no automatic right to strike children any more. The proper exercise of parental authority is the test, and depends on interpretation, but the definition is meant to limit punishment to a measured and moderate action by parents. It can even include hitting a child with something other than a hand. In 2003, for example, a father beat his teenage son several times with a leather belt on the legs with a duvet in between the belt and the skin as the boy would not get out of bed to go to school and had been involved in drugs and dishonesty. The father was acquitted of a charge of assault at the sheriff court.

If after separation the mother has the children, does she have to let the father see them?

Married parents have equal parental rights in law. If there is a dispute, however, then a court can be asked to make orders that regulate when each parent can be with the child, or what responsibilities each shall have. Technically each parent could claim total residence of the child, but obviously that would lead to an impasse, requiring the court to decide. If a parent leaves the matrimonial home, he or she can return at any time, if not prevented by a court order (interdict or exclusion order) and visit or uplift a child. If the child lives in a house to which a parent has no right of entry or occupation (for example, if the mother has moved to a rented flat or a refuge) the parent has no right to go in to see or remove the child.

If an absent or separated parent does not see his children, does he have to pay maintenance?

Yes, if the parent is assessed as being liable to pay by the Child Support Agency or the court. Contact (access) and maintenance do *not* depend on each other.

If a parent does not pay maintenance, can he still insist on seeing a child?

This is the other side of the coin. The law does not make payment of support a precondition for contact (access). However, if an absent parent is trying to seek a court order for contact, then the court will wonder how committed the parent is to the child's welfare if they are not prepared to pay for their upkeep.

Who gets the children if there is a court battle for them?

The principle applied by courts in deciding the welfare, residence of, or parental contact with a child is the best interests of the child. It is not enough for a parent just to love a child or be able to pay for their keep. If the parent has nothing substantial to give the child, or his or her lifestyle, personality or conduct is likely to be harmful to the child, then contact may be refused or limited. There are a range of options open to a court in deciding on the care of a child. For example, the mother may have residence of the child, but the father has contact every Monday after school, every second weekend from Friday until Sunday, two weeks' holiday in the summer, one week at Easter, and alternating Christmas and Boxing days year about. If there is doubt about a parent's ability to cope with childcare, he or she may be supervised by another family member or the other parent. In some areas of Scotland there are contact centres where professional carers provide rooms and assistance in the most difficult contact cases. All orders of the court can be varied (changed) later if circumstances alter. The court will only make an order if it is necessary to do so, or where it is better to make an order than not to make an order. For example, the court may consider that the parents are in need of guidance rather than an instruction, so the sheriff may continue a case for some weeks to give them an opportunity to come to a bilateral agreement, if it is thought they are capable of making the necessary adjustments in contact arrangements without needing the threat of court sanctions. The court has to decide what is in the best interests of the children. This may be something very different from what one or both parents want. The sheriff is impartial and will listen to both parties at hearings, and may get a report from an independent solicitor or social worker, or even a child psychologist, to assist.

How are the interests of the children protected?

In a court case, the principle guiding the sheriff is to decide what is best for the child. Usually both parents claim they know this and are trying to achieve it, but they disagree with each other's judgment. So the sheriff or judge may decide in favour of one parent or the other, or may impose an order for contact, residence, or a mixture of the two, which is different from what either side wants. The sheriff is an experienced judge who knows the law and applies it along with knowledge of family life and human nature to get what he or she considers to be the best result for these children. Cases are fought like battles with two opposing sides, but the sheriff need not just let one side 'win'. The child may have his or her own solicitor, a safeguarder; or a *curator ad litem*, a solicitor that looks after the interests of the child in court, may be involved.

How are the wishes of the children made known?

As long as a child is able to understand what is happening in his or her life and family, the court must ask if they wish to express their views, and, if they do, must listen to those views and take them into account. The sheriff can speak directly to the child or get a report from an independent solicitor, social worker, psychologist or other professional to find this out. The court will not automatically carry out the child's wishes, especially if it feels there may be a parent influencing the child to say what he or she wants. Once a child is aged 12, he or she has specific legal rights: to sue a parent for maintenance, and also to be an independent party in any family court case between his or her parents, with his or her own solicitor.

What if one parent goes to live in another area (of the United Kingdom) and takes the child?

If there are no court orders in place, then there is nothing to stop the parent with the child moving house to wherever he or she wishes. If the other parent doesn't find out until after the move, then he or she must make the best of it, unless he or she thinks that it is necessary for the child's best interests to have the court interfere. It will normally be the court local to the child's residence that is involved: for example, if the move is south of the border, the local English civil court. If that parent finds out in advance, then he can choose to seek an interdict from the court (the one local to where the child is before the move) to prevent the removal of the child. However, this is a sledgehammer tactic, and will only be appropriate if there is some harm or dramatic adverse result likely to happen to the child as a result of the move away. If the parent just wants the child close to him or her, this will not be a sufficient reason. There are plenty of court orders and informal agreements for contact which see one parent travelling long distances for visits with a child. It may be that contact is allowed for longer periods but at longer intervals. A child may come back to the parent's home for holidays rather than weekly visits. If there is already a contact order in place, then this can be enforced (not just in Scotland), though if the circumstances have changed by way of the move, a court can be asked by either parent to review and change the existing order to deal with the new circumstances. As ever, it is the child's best interests that determine what the court does. Note that to enforce a contact order by a Scottish court it must be registered in the part of the United Kingdom that the child is resident in.

What if a parent abducts a child or takes him or her away without the other parent's consent?

Abduction is the removal of a person (in this case a child) by means of force or fraud without that person's consent and without lawful excuse. The police can arrest the abductor and return the child to their rightful parent. It is also an offence to remove a child from someone who has had the care and control of a child for at least three years and has applied to court for a residence order. However, where abduction is by a parent who has parental rights, the removal will not automatically be a crime. It could, however, have civil consequences. No person may remove a child under 16 years of age from someone who has a lawful right of residence or contact. The consent of both parents is required for removal or retention of a child from the United Kingdom.

What if one parent won't tell the other where a child is?

The court has power to force the parent (or any person whom it believes has information, such as to the child's location or the address of the parent) to disclose the whereabouts of the child or information to the court.

How can abduction be prevented?

A parent or someone lawfully caring for a child can seek an interdict from the sheriff court or Court of Session prohibiting the child's removal from the United Kingdom or from any part of it. A person seeking the care of a child can also make the application. The Court of Session has the power to order the surrender of a passport. If a person has reason to suspect that someone else intends to remove a child imminently, they can apply via the police for a 'port stop order' which causes HM Customs and Excise to alert all airports and seaports to watch out for the child (note that the police should be provided with a recent photo of the child to assist the process).

How can an abducted child be recovered or returned?

Scottish courts can be asked to issue a warrant to sheriff officers or messengers-at-arms to search for an abducted child, which can involve breaking down doors and physically seizing the child. The court can issue a delivery order. If the child has been taken abroad then the Hague Child Abduction Convention 1980 has provided a mechanism for return orders. The person seeking the child back can lodge a petition at the Court of Session seeking to establish that wrongful removal or retention has taken place, from a place where the child had his or her habitual residence, and note that residence cannot be changed by one parent acting unilaterally. There is no strict time limit on this procedure, but if it takes more than one year after removal, then the child need not be returned if he or she has settled into their new residence. There is a defence for the abducting parent that if the child is returned then the child will be at grave risk of being exposed to physical or psychological harm, or be placed in an intolerable situation. This is, however, rarely a successful defence as the courts have set very strict standards for proving this. The court will listen to the views of the child if they are of an age and maturity to warrant this. It is fair to say that these cases often involve substantial emotional and cultural conflict and both parents genuinely feeling they can offer what is best for the child. The court equally has power under the Hague Convention to recognise rights of access to children, make orders and ensure existing ones are enforced, and fix conditions for the exercise of the orders if they are being obstructed.

What are the legal requirements for education of a child?

A child of school age (between the ages of 5 and 16 years) is entitled to a sufficient education. The law says the parent(s) must ensure that children receive efficient education by sending them to school 'or by other means', which can include education at home if it meets appropriate standards. A parent is guilty of a criminal offence if the child fails, without reasonable excuse, to attend school. 'Reasonable excuse' can be illness, lack of adequate transport (a child should not have to walk more than three miles, or two miles if the child is under eight years old) or genuine family reasons like bereavement, or religious observance.

What punishments can a school or teacher legally administer?

Along with parents, teachers have traditionally had a common law right of reasonable physical chastisement. However, while teachers are immune from prosecution in the criminal courts for such behaviour, they can now be sued in the civil courts. It is unlikely now that any teacher would strike a pupil as they may lose their job and could even be sued by the child. If a teacher were to use the belt or the cane on a child now, they would commit a criminal as well as a civil wrong, as this would not be reasonable chastisement. An alternative punishment is to exclude the child from school. To lawfully exclude the child certain conditions have to be satisfied and procedures followed. The child or his parents still have rights of appeal against the exclusion. Detention after the closure of school may also be enforced as a punishment, within reason and subject to parental consent. Lines can be demanded from the child. These should have an educational content. Alternatively, a teacher may choose to withdraw some or all of a child's privileges while at school. A teacher may temporarily confiscate dangerous or disruptive objects in the child's possession. It may be appropriate to refer a child to the Reporter to the Children's Panel for non-attendance or for other concerning behaviour. This, however, should not be regarded as a punishment, but rather as a means for helping and protecting the child.

What is adoption?

Adoption is a legal process by which a new relationship of parent and child is legally created by court. This is much more fundamental than residence and contact orders, as it does not just give parents the rights and duties of looking after children in their care, but makes them full members of the new family. An adopted child is legally entitled to succeed to the adoptive parent's estate on the parent's death. The natural parents of the child lose all parental rights as a result of the adoption. Sometimes the new spouse of a natural parent will adopt the child of their partner. If so, the natural parent does not need to adopt his or her own child. Both become equal parents, giving them every right and duty of parents, including responsibility for maintenance of the child.

How can a child be adopted?

Adoption is a court process taken at the sheriff court. A child is adopted through a legal adoption agency, either a local authority or an approved adoption society, or privately. Private adoptions, however, are only legal if they are of children related to the adopter or as a result of placement by a Children's Panel. The child must be not younger than 19 weeks and not older than 18 years (unless the application was commenced before the child turned 18). The adoptive parents make a formal application to court for adoption, and various court procedures can then take place. The adoption can only be made when the court is satisfied that each parent or guardian of the child agrees to it. If there is opposition from any of these parties, the court will consider the opposition, and, if satisfied that it is appropriate for adoption to proceed, it can free the child for adoption by dispensing with the agreement. If the child is 12 years or over the consent of the child must also be sought. Once all the procedural steps are out of the way, the sheriff will grant the adoption order if satisfied that it is in the best interests of the child's welfare. On reaching the age of 16 years adopted children are entitled to information in respect of their birth, family and origin. They can be enabled to trace their original birth registration entry. Counselling services are made available to them.

What rights do the natural parents have after adoption?

None by law, but on rare occasions they may be allowed limited contact, sometimes by oblique means such as passing on birthday presents or cards via a relative.

Where is the adoption registered?

In the Adopted Children's Register maintained by local authorities.

Can a parent change a child's name and get this registered?

If you were born or adopted in Scotland, you can record a change of name with the Registrar General. You can obtain the appropriate application form from any Registrar of Births, Deaths and Marriages in Scotland or the Change of Name unit of the Registrar General's Office. A change of forename(s) or surname(s) cannot be recorded unless evidence is produced that the name has been in use for at least two years. For a child under two years, any alternative forename must be in use prior to the child's first birthday. An application to record the change must be made before the child's second birthday. No additional evidence is required other than the completed application form. Only one change of forename(s) and one change of surname(s) may be recorded for a child under 16 years of age. For a child under the age of two, only a change of forename(s) may be recorded.

What if the other parent objects?

The naming of a child in contentious circumstances can be taken up at court as a matter of parental responsibilities. It would be up to the parent wanting to contest the matter to show that it is in the best interests of the child to change the name or retain a changed name if challenged by the other parent. The court would look at the child's present life to see whether a new name suits the family unit and relationships he or she has.

How does the law deal with children who criminally offend?

The age of criminal responsibility is eight years. Children under 16 years of age who are alleged to have committed an offence are usually dealt with by the Children's Panel. For exceptional cases, a child can be prosecuted in the (adult) High Court or the sheriff court. If a child is under 16 years when an alleged offence is committed but 16 years or over when prosecution is commenced, then the Procurator Fiscal can proceed in the adult court.

How do children end up in care?

If a child is at risk in their present home or environment they can be taken into care. The local authority has the legal duty to safeguard and promote the welfare of local children who are in need. As well as assistance of various kinds, the authority has the power to provide accommodation for a child under 18 years if either no one has parental responsibility for the child, the child is lost or abandoned or the child's usual carer cannot provide the child with suitable accommodation or care. The authority also has the power to exclude an abusive parent from a home to allow the child to remain there safely rather than taking the child away. A child may also be considered to need compulsory measures of care. This is usually arranged through the social work department and the Reporter to the Children's Panel. The local authority can apply to the sheriff court for an order transferring parental rights and responsibilities to the authority. Such orders are granted only if there is no practical or suitable alternative. The child must be consulted as part of the process. Emergency child protection orders can be sought from the court to deal with a crisis in which the child is in urgent need of care.

What does the Children's Panel do?

The Children's Panel or Hearing can make a range of decisions for children referred to it for committing offences. If guilt is admitted or proved the Children's Panel can impose a range of orders, including home supervision, and, in extreme cases, detention in secure accommodation. These channels are not, however, just for offenders. Children who are abused or neglected can be brought before the Panel in order for appropriate measures to be taken to keep them safe.

Can a child have a lawyer of his or her own?

A child under the age of 16 may instruct his or her own solicitor if considered capable of understanding the proceedings. Generally, a child of 12 years will be considered of sufficient maturity. A child may be represented in a Children's Panel Hearing, in criminal court or in a civil action (such as divorce actions). If a child is too young to understand the proceedings, a *curator ad litem* may be appointed by the court. The duty of this lawyer will be to safeguard the child's best interests. The main obstacle to a child having legal representation in civil proceedings and children's hearings is the availability of legal aid. It is important to remember that the solicitor will act for the child, and not just do what the parents say or want.

What rights and legal powers do children have?

A child under 16 year of age cannot enter a legally binding transaction (other than a routine one, such as the purchase of sweets or small retail goods); make a binding promise; or witness a signature. A child can, however, own property. A child aged 12 can make a will; act as an executor in a will; and consent to a freeing for adoption order. A child can consent to any medical treatment as long as the doctor considers that he or she understands the nature and possible consequences of the treatment. A doctor should not try to circumvent the child's consent or lack of it by going to the parents; only the court can overrule the child's wishes. Children can be liable in damages if they had a sufficient understanding that their actions were wrong or harmful. Children can give evidence in court at any age as long as they understand what they are doing and know the difference between truth and falsehood, though if they are younger they may not be asked to take the witness oath.

What happens if a man is accused of being the father of a child and denies it? Or what if a man claims paternity and this is denied by the mother?

The law provides a mechanism for establishing paternity. It is easily done by blood and DNA testing, but you cannot force someone to undergo such testing in the civil law (see chapter 13 on the procedure for police to take samples). Either parent, or the child involved, can go to court to seek a declarator of paternity. This is an order judicially recognising the man as the father. This may be relevant for child support purposes, or for inheritance to a parent's estate on death, or even to prove adultery in a divorce case. If a man refuses to submit to DNA testing, a court may in some cases be entitled to make a presumption about his paternity if there is other consistent evidence. Note that a husband is presumed to be the father of a child born during the marriage.

What provision does the law make for gay parents?

The guiding principle in the law affecting children is that whatever is in the best interests of children should be done. This should underpin the resolution of any dispute about whether a child should see or live with a particular parent. The law does not have a specific category or rulebook for gay parents any more than it does for disabled parents, foreign parents or parents wearing glasses. Gay mothers and fathers have the same rights and responsibilities as all parents in Scotland do. On the assumption that the most likely cause of legal dispute is that one parent does not want the other (gay) parent to have any or more contact with or residence of a child, then it is up to the court to be satisfied that the parent loves the child, is able to look after it and benefit its life, and that there is no circumstance that would be harmful to the child. Sex or sexuality is only relevant if it is the cause or the effect of a harmful home environment that the child should be kept from.

Is it legal to arrange a surrogate pregnancy, and whose baby is it?

Surrogacy, the birth of a baby by a substitute mother using the sperm of a childless couple, is lawful. Indeed, a court can be asked to grant a parental order which provides for the child who is the result of a surrogacy arrangement to be treated as the child of the couple who sought the surrogacy. The couple must be married, the pregnancy must have been by other than natural conception, and the application to court must be made within six months of birth. There are other conditions, including that the court must be sure that no fee was paid to the surrogate mother other than expenses. Paying for a surrogacy remains illegal.

Landmark ages for children

12	Buy a pet
14	Have a part-time job (restricted hours); go into a pub with an adult to consume soft drinks
16	Obtain a motor bike licence; obtain a provisional driving licence; leave school, work full-time; claim social security benefits in own right; join a trade union; buy cigarettes; buy lottery tickets; get married; engage in heterosexual sex; engage in a homosexual act; join the armed forces; consume wine, cider or beer with a meal in a restaurant
17	Drive a car
18	Vote; be on jury service; be hypnotised on stage; work in licensed premises; gamble; buy alcohol; get a tattoo
21	Sit as an MP or MSP; obtain an HGV licence

Chapter 4

Domestic Violence

A. LAFFERTY

Please note: In this chapter, purely for the sake of economy of space, I have made the husband or male partner the abuser, and the wife or female the victim. The law is, however, neutral, that is both sexes have the right to the same protections as the other, as there are women who are violent and abusive to men. So the genders can be read interchangeably in these questions and answers.

What can an abused wife do in law to prevent violence or threats?

Any assault or threat on a spouse is unlawful. It may be a crime, and can be reported to the police. The obstacle here is often the proof. A prosecution for assault requires evidence from two sources, and often there are no witnesses to abuse apart from the victim and the perpetrator, and the perpetrator has the right of silence. Under civil matrimonial law, however, a course of violence or intimidating behaviour to a spouse or children allows the victim to seek various protective court orders, including exclusion from the house of the perpetrator; suspension of his occupancy rights in the house; interdict/exclusion against him returning; other interdicts against him interfering with the victim, the children or family property; and a power of arrest, that allows the police to arrest the perpetrator and lock him up if he even show his face at the house without consent. These are dealt with in more detail below.

What if there are no other witnesses to the abuse?

If the court is satisfied, on a balance of probabilities, that the abuse has taken place as stated then the orders will be made. If there is medical evidence of injuries, then that will bolster the single-witness evidence. The victim can also bring evidence from family members in whom she has confided or evidence of the abuser being violent to others. The main thing is that an abused person should not be put off from seeking to enforce her rights by giving up before she starts. Sometimes the very process of exposing a violent partner is enough to make them stop the abuse or leave.

How does the law protect a spouse from matrimonial violence or abuse?

In the old days a husband could lawfully put his wife out of the house if she was not on the title deeds or the lease for the house. In addition, if there were no independent witnesses to an assault, he could usually get away without being prosecuted for beating her. From 1980 this changed: as well as bringing in the provision of occupancy rights for a non-entitled spouse mentioned above, the Matrimonial Homes (Family Protection) (Scotland) Act 1981 created new powers for the courts to deal with victims of abuse. This law has been refined a couple of times since then, and presently there is fairly comprehensive protection available for battered, abused or threatened spouses (both husbands and wives) and children. I use the word available, as sadly there is often still an ignorance of the basic rights to which victims of domestic violence are entitled, and a reluctance, firstly, to acknowledge what is happening in the house, secondly, to share the facts with friends or family, and, thirdly, to take the necessary legal steps to get help. However, once the victim takes the plunge, a solicitor can go to court on her behalf to seek emergency (interim) orders to do one or more of the following (amongst others):

- **Interdict** (this is equivalent to the English law term Injunction): this is an order for the abuser to *stop* his misconduct and refrain from repeating it. If he breaks this order he can be punished for contempt of court by a fine or even imprisonment.
- **Interdict**: against the perpetrator removing children or interfering with their care.
- **Exclusion**: this makes him leave the house.
- **Suspension of occupancy rights**: this temporarily takes away his right to live in the house.

- **Power of arrest**: this order, which can be granted for up to three years at a time, allows the victim to call the police if the interdicted abuser breaks the court orders or even turns up unannounced at the matrimonial home. If the power of arrest has been granted by the court and made known to the police, they are obliged on information received from the abused spouse to come to the home and arrest the abuser, even if he is not committing a criminal offence or if there are no other witnesses than the victim. They will take him into custody pending a court appearance, usually the next working day.

It is worth stressing that part of the victimisation process in an abusive relationship is the fear of taking action as either this will be unsuccessful or make matters worse. The law, however, has been specifically designed to do two main things: to get even the worst and most dangerous abuser out of and away from the house, and to give the abused spouse and the children security to live in peace in their own home. It does need a little bit of determination to make the decision to take legal steps, but, if there is no other way, then it is worth it. Legal aid is available to those who qualify financially. The emergency steps can be taken by a solicitor within days; sometimes action can be taken and even a court hearing arranged the very same day the victim consults a solicitor. These powers can be invoked by a victim either on their own, or within a divorce action.

How does the law deal with domestic violence in an unmarried partnership?

See the earlier question and answer on domestic violence in marriage; many of the points are the same for couples living together. At the present time, however, there are further legal hoops for victimised unmarried partners to go through. The interdicts, exclusion orders and powers of arrest provided by the law are based on the 'occupancy rights' of the abused partner. Not everyone living in someone else's house has such rights. To secure them, a partner needs to ask the court to grant a Declarator of Occupancy Rights. In effect you need to persuade the court that you have established residence in your partner's house as your home. The length of residence, intentions of the parties and financial dependence may be some of the factors considered towards proving your case. The Declarator is a legal certificate of occupancy. It is granted for a fixed period and can be renewed, and is the key that allows the enforcement and protection orders to be granted for you and your children if needed. Again, legal aid is available if you financially qualify. See also chapter 3.

Chapter 5

Neighbours and Privacy

Can my neighbours or I do more or less what we like in our own homes?

No! There is a broad legal rule that everyone is bound to use his or her property so as not to injure or annoy his or her neighbour. Neighbours can cause legal nuisance by keeping noisy or smelly animals, causing loud noise and vibrations, polluting the air or water, or activities that are generally incompatible with peaceful coexistence. Whether specific behaviour amounts to nuisance depends upon all the circumstances, including the type of the conduct and the nature of the neighbourhood in which it occurs. To be labelled 'nuisance', the conduct or behaviour must be considered unreasonable, and cause actual harm, inconvenience or discomfort. What may be acceptable in an industrial estate may not be acceptable in a suburban residential place.

What do I do if I have noisy or nuisance neighbours?

First, you should attempt to reason with your neighbour and reach a friendly agreement. If this does not work, there are remedies in the criminal and civil law. In cases of excessive noise you may contact the police or the environmental health department of your local authority who have statutory powers to prevent continuing disturbance. You could instead, or as well, instruct your solicitor to raise civil court proceedings for an interdict. This is a sheriff court order to your neighbour to make him stop causing the nuisance. If the problem is urgent, the sheriff can award an interim interdict within a day or two. If your neighbour is a tenant, you could complain to his landlord who could then go to court to evict the tenant, as his misbehaviour would amount to non-compliance with his tenancy agreement. It is possible to sue your neighbour for financial damages only if their conduct has caused actual injury, that is, damage to your property, or physical or psychological injury to you.

What can the police do about bad neighbours?

The police can use the criminal law to solve the problem of nuisance neighbours. For example, the misconduct (such as excessive noise or creating noxious smells) may constitute a statutory offence, that is, one created by an Act of Parliament. The police have powers in some Acts to deal with those who cause such nuisance. The police could alternatively charge your neighbour with the common law crime of breach of the peace. This is essentially a minor offence with a broad definition, and can include threatening behaviour, noisy parties and the deliberate production of noise.

What can the local authority do about bad neighbours?

Environmental health officers from your local council have the power to serve an abatement notice upon those who are responsible for the creation of excessive noise. This orders your neighbour to stop causing the nuisance within a specified time. The local authority is obliged to investigate every complaint of statutory nuisance. They can then decide whether it is appropriate to serve a notice and/or take other legal action. The local authority or the police may apply to the sheriff court for an Anti-social Behaviour Order. This prohibits your neighbour from doing anything that is described in the order as anti-social. If your neighbour were to breach the order, he would be guilty of a criminal offence and could then be prosecuted. If your neighbour is a local authority tenant, the council, as their landlord, can seek to evict in extreme cases (many councils have transferred their housing stock to other bodies, so it is those bodies who would have this right). You can also personally serve a statutory nuisance notice instead of relying upon the local authority to do so. You can also consult a solicitor for help to complete a notice.

I am afraid I will be targeted if I report my neighbours. What protection do I have?

✗ The Anti-social Behaviour Order, mentioned above, can be sought from a court if your neighbours are harassing you or causing you alarm or distress that is likely to continue. If a violent incident occurs you should, of course, contact the police. Your neighbour may be charged with breach of the peace or assault. You could raise an action of 'harassment' if your neighbour has behaved in a way that has caused you alarm or distress on at least two occasions. This can include threatening phone calls. The court may award damages and grant an interdict or a non-harassment order. A non-harassment order would require your neighbour to refrain from the conduct that is alarming you. If your neighbour acts in breach of this order, he will be guilty of a criminal offence. You should not goad a neighbour to get him into trouble as this would be provocation and would lessen his blame.

What officials have the right to enter my house and whom can I refuse to let in?

The basic rule is that you have the right to privacy and the sanctity of your own home. There are, however, a great many exceptions to this. They say an Englishman's home is his castle; this is not true in England, and equally inaccurate in Scotland. You can refuse entry to your home to private individuals, salesmen, debt collectors and anyone without specific legal authority to come in (which usually means an official person who has an official warrant or court order to come in). Even police officers cannot enter unless they have a warrant (properly granted by a court) to enter your premises for the purpose of search or arrest, or are in hot pursuit of a suspect, or if drugs or property would likely be removed or destroyed while a warrant is applied for. They can also come in to quell a disturbance, enforce an arrest warrant, or if they hear cries for help. There must be some reasonable cause to entitle them to act immediately. Other officials also have powers: the fire service has the right to enter to deal with fire or suspected fire and water companies can enter if there is an emergency. Many other officials can enter, but only with a warrant, such as the taxman if he suspects a serious evasion offence is taking place.

Do we have a law of trespass?

Trespass is a recognised civil wrong in Scots law. It is not generally criminal conduct, though there is now a statutory offence of aggravated trespass. Genetic modification crop protesters in the Black Isle were the first convicted of the crime in Scotland in 2003. Trespass is the temporary intrusion into the property of another without the permission of the owner or lawful occupier, who can go to court for an interdict to prevent further trespasses. You can only claim financial damages if there has been damage done to your property by the intruder.

What can I do if a neighbour parks his car or otherwise obstructs my driveway?

You have a right of access to your land. The local authority and the police have extensive powers to tow vehicles that are illegally parked, causing an obstruction on the highway or which are abandoned. However, you may not wish to consult officials immediately. It is best to talk reasonably to your neighbour in the first instance to avoid unnecessary intervention and to try and keep the peace. If you think you might lose your temper, it may be best to write a letter. If the car is parked in the street, but is blocking the entrance to your driveway, this is a form of nuisance. If this happens on more than one occasion, you could instruct your solicitor to seek an interdict. This would also be appropriate if the obstruction is caused by something other than a vehicle. If your neighbour parked his car in your driveway or on another part of your land, this would constitute trespass.

My neighbour has a tree that overhangs my garden; can I get him to keep the branches cut back?

If your neighbour will not keep the trees or bushes in trim you are entitled to lop the branches off at the line of your property, and return the cut limbs to them.

My neighbour is building an extension that will cut down my light and be built right up against my property. Can I stop this?

He should of course have, in many cases, applied for planning permission and served a copy of the application on you as a neighbour, which would have given you the right to object to the local planning authority, who are duty bound to take your interests into account in deciding on his application. If it is granted, then your position is limited. You do not have a right of appeal against this grant of planning permission. You should check your title deeds and your neighbours'; there may be a restriction on such developments, or you may have rights of prospect or light (though these are unusual and unlikely to be stated). If all else fails, you can perhaps prevent him going ahead if he needs access on to your property to carry out the building work; he has no right to access and you can stop him if he tries.

My neighbour's children run amok around our house/ garden/lane and have damaged property. Can I sue their parents?

No, all you can do is report the children to the police if their conduct is more than just high-spirited play and becomes vandalism or breach of the peace. It will generally, however, take a lot to get police to treat young children as criminals, but at least they may speak to the parents and get through to them more effectively than you, as an ordinary neighbour, can.

Chapter 6

A Home of Your Own

A.LAFFERTY

What are title deeds?

A Land Certificate is effectively your title deed. It is the ownership document issued by the Land Register of Scotland that proves your ownership of land. The Register is backed up by computer records in case you lose your copy of the Land Certificate. This system of Land Registration is replacing the Sasine recording of deeds, which has its roots in the feudal system of the middle ages.

What is meant by conveyancing?

Conveyancing is the process of property transfer. The conveyancing sequence usually starts when a written contract (missives) is concluded between the seller and purchaser; a title deed is then drawn up and signed by the seller in favour of the purchaser; the title deed is then delivered to the purchaser in exchange for the price, and finally it is registered. The purchaser takes possession (entry) at the time the price is paid. The transaction usually also involves searches to make sure that there are no orders preventing the transaction proceeding, and reports on the property and the ground underneath it. The solicitors for the two parties handle all this.

What are missives?

The word just means something sent, as in mission or missile. The usual routine is that the purchaser's solicitor types up an offer, containing details of the proposed price, date of entry, contents, and a host of detailed legal conditions designed to protect the interests of the purchaser. The seller's lawyer copies it on to his or her client, and takes instructions as to the seller's agreement or otherwise to the terms. The lawyer will then send a written acceptance: usually this will not be a simple acceptance, but one qualified by proposals to change or delete unacceptable clauses in the offer; hence the term 'qualified acceptance' which you will hear solicitors use. The purchaser then must decide if he wants to accept or reject those counter-conditions. Once all matters are agreed in writing, there is conclusion of missives and thus a mutually binding contract.

Are builders' missives different?

Yes, as traditionally larger builders and construction companies who build new housing developments try to issue uniform missives or house sale agreements.

What are the usual legal costs involved in buying and selling houses?

It is a substantial expense to get conveyancing work done. To correct a common misconception, however, lawyers do not get all, or even most, of what you have to pay out. The bulk goes, one way or another, to the government. In purchases, you pay a solicitor's fee (which is a negotiable figure and can be agreed in advance), with VAT on top of that (which goes to the state). If your property is being bought for more than £60,000, you have Stamp Duty Land Tax to pay (to the government again), at either 1% of the whole price up to £250,000, or 3% if the price is more than that, and registration dues charged by the Land Register of Scotland on a sliding scale (and sliding right into the government's bank account). On a sale, you have solicitor's fee, then outlays for property enquiry reports, title searches and even mining reports, plus a registration outlay if you are paying off a mortgage on the house being sold. The rates and combinations of figures make it impractical to show you examples of the overall costs of conveyancing (and don't forget you will have survey fees and estate agent's fees to factor in), but it is a requirement for Scottish solicitors that you are provided with an accurate breakdown of costs in writing at the outset of a transaction you are instructing.

Can either party get out of the contract to sell or buy a house if he changes his mind?

After missives are concluded, even though this may be weeks or months before the date for payment of the price (date of entry or settlement), neither party can get out, unless some legal problem arises which is agreed in the missives as a reason to allow the party out (resile from the bargain). In the absence of such a reason, there are hefty financial penalties for defaulting, as it constitutes a breach of contract.

I have heard gazumping is not possible in Scotland; is that true?

The English form of gazumping cannot happen in Scotland, that is where a couple of days before completion of the transaction one party threatens to back out if the other party does not pay more money, or does back out when another purchaser comes along with a better price. In Scotland, conclusion of missives means that both parties are bound to the transaction when all terms are agreed, usually within a week or so of the original offer being made, and if one wants to back out or change things, the other can sue them to enforce the contract. Before missives are concluded there is nothing to stop either party backing out or holding a gun to the other's head if he chooses to do so. However, a demand for more money in the price or a change in the terms of the contract could result in the purchaser calling the bluff and leaving the seller with no purchaser at all.

How can I be sure the house I am buying is both physically and legally sound?

Your solicitor makes sure that the seller provides clear searches against the property in the Land Register of Scotland or Register of Sasines, and also that the seller is free of any court orders like inhibition (which is an order placed on the public register), or sequestration (which puts all of the owner's property in the hands of an appointed trustee); either of which would prevent them having right to sell. Also the seller is made to show clear property enquiry reports that there are no local authority repair orders or planning permission problems on the house, and a clear mining report that there are no underground problems from old mines known about. Also if there have been alterations to the house, your solicitor should ensure the seller provides the correct paperwork for them.

Who is responsible if something goes wrong in a house sale or purchase?

If your solicitor has missed something that costs you money, he or she may be liable to you for negligence. If the other party has failed to provide something you are entitled to, you can seek compensation from that party for your reasonable losses.

What if my surveyor missed something wrong with the house when inspecting or surveying?

Again, the surveyor has a professional duty to persons entitled to rely upon his or her expertise. If a mistake is made which should have been avoided, you may have a claim against the surveyor company. However, be aware that surveyors can put in reasonable get-out clauses in their contract with you, and also there are various types of survey from a basic valuation to an in-depth inspection. The more you ask for and pay for, the better your protection.

Should I sell first or buy first?

This depends on market forces at the time. If you are confident your own house will sell easily, you may be better to buy first. If you do so, then whether or not you have sold or got an offer for your own house, you may have to conclude missives for the purchase of the new one, and hope that you get an offer for your own property in time. If you have a date of entry for your purchase that falls before your sale date, you may have to get a bridging loan from a bank for the whole purchase price, or else for the whole price less the new mortgage (though not all lenders will allow you to utilise your new mortgage before you sell your old house and repay your old mortgage). If by the time your date of entry for purchase comes around you have not at least concluded missives for your own sale, very few lenders or banks will allow you open-ended bridging, and if you cannot secure the funds for the purchase, you will not be able to pay, and you will be in breach of the contract of purchase. Usually the missives allow you a period of grace to get the money (three weeks from the date of entry is normal) but if you cannot pay by then, the seller is free to re-sell the house to another person. You would then have to pay both interest on the unpaid price, any shortfall if it has to be re-sold for less, and also any additional expenses the seller has had, such as legal expenses and removal or storage costs. Most cautious people will sell first, and if you have not bought a new house by the time you move out of your own (remember as your sale is a binding contract, the purchaser is entitled to move into yours if they pay the price on the entry date) then you will have to go into temporary accommodation and store your furniture.

How do I get the best mortgage deal?

You can take advice from a lender such as a bank, building society or other mortgage company, or you can speak to your solicitor if he or she is capable of giving this advice or is registered under the Financial Services Act (you can check this when you instruct him or her), or you can engage a professional mortgage broker or independent financial adviser. Be careful, shop around and try to get as much information from the adviser as possible.

What documents and permissions do I need to alter or extend my house?

Any work that changes the structure of the house needs a building warrant before the work is done, and a completion certificate after it is finished, to show it is authorised and satisfactory to the local authority building control department. If the work is done without that procedure, then a purchaser can back out of a transaction when the problem comes to light. You can ask building control for a letter of comfort to be granted, saying that although the proper certificates have not been applied for or issued, the council are satisfied with the work and they will not insist on remedial action. If not done well, the council can insist on the house being put back as it was or remedial work being done. If something is being done that changes the appearance of the house, planning permission may also be required. And if the title deeds so dictate, an owner may have to get the permission of the superior, who may be the developer if the site is modern or the former landlord of the feudal estate on which the property is built.

Can I alter or extend my house without the neighbour's permission?

If you are doing something that requires planning permission then, as part of the application, you will need to give a neighbour notification form to all neighbours adjoining and within a set distance. They then have the right to object to the council, who will take any objections into account when deciding on your application. The objections from neighbours can range from the claim that it will block his light, look ghastly or that the extension is too near his property.

If I want to build a wall or fence do I need planning permission?

If the proposed wall or fence in a back garden does not exceed six feet, or in a front garden three feet, you do not need planning permission.

Can I get access on to my neighbour's property to maintain my own property or build a boundary wall?

No. Unless your title deeds give you specific permission to go on to neighbouring land for maintenance or repair, you have no right to cross the border. A boundary fence needs to be totally inside your own land.

Can I buy my council house?

If you have been a tenant of the local authority or certain public authorities for five years, you can do so. You are entitled to a discount depending on the length of tenancy, with no distinction as there was previously between houses and flats. Discounts start at 20% and increase by 1% per year up to a *maximum* of 35% or £15,000 whichever is lower. Certain types of property are excluded: for example, some houses tied to employment such as caretakers' houses. If you are in arrears with council tax or rent, your sale can be suspended until this is paid off. After you have accepted the council's offer to sell in writing, you must retain the house for three years. You can make an application to buy to the council who will have the property valued, and will issue a legal offer. You are entitled to correspond with the seller on your own, but the transaction has legal consequences and involves conveyancing, so you are best consulting a solicitor.

What if I want to re-sell my council house within three years?

If you sell or transfer the house to someone else before the end of three years, you will have to repay all or part of the discount sum. Once you are issued with an offer to sell, you must give written acceptance within two months or the offer will lapse. If you sell the house or transfer it away within the first year after you accept the offer to sell, you will have to repay the whole discount to the council. If you sell within two years, it's 66% to be repaid; three years, 33%. After three years' owner-occupation you can sell or transfer the property with no clawback. Also, if you die before the three years are up, the house can be sold by your executor without any clawback.

Can I buy my council house and put someone else on the title deeds?

The local authority will only sell to the tenant or joint tenants and members of the immediate family who have lived in the property as their actual residence for the qualifying period. If you transfer to another family member or to a third party before three years after acceptance of the offer to sell by the authority, all or part of the discount will be clawed back as above.

What if I have a house and want to transfer it to my family?

There is nothing to stop you doing that (though if you have bought your local/public authority house, you must wait three years after accepting the offer to sell, or else part of the discount on the price will be clawed back by the selling authority), but see the next question . . .

What if I have to go into a care home and I have a house? Will the council take it off me for the care home fees?

This is a minefield. If you have to go into care or sheltered housing, and seek benefits or public funding for costs of accommodation, then you will be assessed to see if you qualify financially. There are capital limits, and if you have more than the allowed amount of capital (including savings, shares, bonds, cash, and property) then you will be turned down. To avoid this problem, some people have transferred savings or a house to members of their family, so that they can say to the funding authority that, at the time of application, they do not have these assets. However, the law presently allows the authority in many cases to look back in time and find out if the applicant owned property in the past. If so, and if the property was transferred for no payment or an artificially reduced payment, then the authority can seek to ignore that transfer and treat the applicant as if they still owned the asset. You may regard it as immoral, that you work all your life, pay taxes and save up or build up a valuable house by your own efforts, only to have it taken away by the State to pay for your old age, but that, to a great extent at the moment, is the law.

If I go into care, can the council or Benefits Agency take my house off me to sell for the care costs?

I am asked this question a lot, but this is not the way the system works. The funding authority will assess you and either accept or reject your application. If you have capital assets the value of which put you above the financial limits for benefit, your application will be refused. Subject to any appeal you may make, rejection means that if you want to stay in the care facility or home, you must pay private fees. Failure to do so can mean eviction, as the home is entitled to its fees. You may have to sell your house or use up other assets to pay the fees. You will then have to use up the proceeds of sale until you have reduced your capital to the level at which you are entitled to receive the benefits. So it is not the council that has any involvement in taking or selling your home; but, in order to pay care home fees, you may need to liquidate this asset to get the cash to pay the home.

Chapter 7

Renting Property

Do I always have the right to a lease document?

For all private tenancies the landlord must provide free of charge a lease or tenancy document stating the terms of the tenancy, and also, where rent is paid weekly, a rent book. But if he does not, then this does not mean you, as a tenant, have no rights. The rights are broadly those which are provided by the law.

What rights does a landlord have?

The landlord of course has the benefit of writing his own lease for new tenants and can specify his rules and requirements, the level of rent, the term or length of the lease and the limitations on the conduct of the tenant and any guests in the premises. However, the law surrounding the commercial letting industry is very detailed and the landlord's freedom of manoeuvre is limited in many ways. Where the tenant has a right given by Parliament, this acts as a duty on the landlord. So read on . . .

What if I am threatened with eviction?

It depends on what grounds the eviction is based. If you have not paid your rent, or you are in some other way in breach of the lease or tenancy, then you may ultimately be evicted. However, the law gives tenants many chances to remedy any breach of contract, and the court often has discretion as to whether to grant a landlord an order to evict you. If you have withheld rent because a flat is unhealthy, a sheriff may be reluctant to evict you (you could on the other hand try to get an order against the landlord for repairs or upgrading to be carried out). Even if you are the worst tenant in the land, you can hold on to possession until the very end of a legal process to evict you.

How can a landlord get rid of a bad tenant?

A landlord can only remove a tenant with a court order. He cannot change the locks or throw a tenant's goods out in the street as that would be a crime. There are different grounds for a landlord to recover possession of property, such as the need to sell the property; moving back in himself as he needs it as a home; for redevelopment; or because the tenant has breached the tenancy by failing to pay the rent, causing damage or disturbance, subletting without permission; or for a whole host of other reasons. Most of these grounds give the court a discretion as to whether to grant eviction or not, but a small number are mandatory grounds which require the sheriff to grant the order. The tenant always has the right to contest an application by the landlord to the court, and eviction cannot be granted until the end of the case. A tenant can apply for legal aid to pay for representation in contesting the eviction, and this can make the case last even longer than it otherwise would. For landlords, the process of getting rid of even the most appalling tenant may be a very long and expensive process indeed. And remember, as well as having the proper grounds for eviction, a landlord must obey the strict procedural rules for service of a notice to quit (and the correct notice at that) or else an eviction may fail for procedural reasons even if you have a good reason to evict.

Can a landlord just come in and change the locks?

No, he commits a serious criminal offence if he does, and you as tenant can just re-enter the property anyway, as your lease has not been properly terminated.

What if a landlord will not return my deposit after the end of the tenancy?

A deposit is paid at the outset of a tenancy, and is normally the equivalent of a month's rent. At the end of the lease, no matter whether it is given up by agreement or by eviction, the deposit should be returned, unless there are actual damages or losses caused by the tenant which can be legitimately offset by retention of the deposit or a part of it. If it is retained unreasonably, the tenant can sue for its return in the small claims court.

Often the dispute is about alleged damages that the tenant says were done before he took entry. Incoming tenants should make a list of faults or damages after a close inspection of the premises *before* moving in.

Can I retain rent if the landlord is in breach of his obligations?

Most tenancy documents make it unlawful and a breach of contract for a tenant to retain rent in any circumstances. If there is no mention of it, the tenant may withhold rent if the landlord is in default of his obligations, such as to the state of the building.

Who pays for repairs?

The tenant must pay for any damage caused by him or those in the property by his permission. But the landlord is responsible for keeping the structure of the building wind and watertight and in good tenantable order. The house must be kept fit for human habitation during the tenancy, and, also the landlord must keep the installations of gas, water, sanitation, electricity, space and water heating in repair. The tenancy document can increase the landlord's obligations by agreement, but cannot reduce them below the legal standard.

Who pays the Council Tax?

The tenant is the occupier in possession of the house and pays the Council Tax.

If I want to vacate the property before the end of the lease can I do so?

A tenancy is not like a job; you cannot just resign with a month's notice given. If the lease says it is for a period or a minimum of, say, six months, then rent has to be paid for that whole time if the landlord insists. The landlord may waive this if there is another tenant available, but this would be his choice and not a legal obligation. If you just leave, then you can be sued for any outstanding rent.

If I rent the property along with others, is the rent shared equally?

If the landlord has entered separate leases with individual tenants, then he can only claim rent from each according to the rent agreed with that tenant. But if there is joint and several liability among tenants, then each will be responsible for the whole rent, and the landlord can claim it from or sue only one, leaving it to that tenant to get back other shares from other co-tenants, if he can.

What if the rented property is damp, unsafe or unhealthy?

There are legal powers under various Acts of Parliament which allow the tenant to go to court to seek an order to be granted forcing a landlord to effect repairs or improvements, and also allow local authorities to do so if there is risk to health or safety. Landlords in multiple-occupancy lets must keep safety logs and fire safety equipment. The Commissioner for Local Administration in Scotland (Local Government Ombudsman) can also be advised of problems; although having no direct power to order remedial work, a failure by the local authority to repair may amount to maladministration by the authority. The tenant can also sue the landlord for damages if the state of the building has caused physical suffering or financial loss.

Chapter 8

Shopping, Consumer Rights and Contracts

Consumer purchases

Can I cancel a purchase or other contract?

Generally, once an agreement is made it is binding on both sides. Even if you realise you have made a mistake or have paid a higher price than you needed to, the contract cannot be set aside unless there was misrepresentation or fraud on the part of the seller. Children making contracts have the right to cancel them in some circumstances as they are presumed to be insufficiently mature to bind themselves to onerous financial commitments.

Is there a cooling-off period for purchases?

Not generally, though if you are sold credit in a place such as your own home, that is not in retail premises you have gone to, you have seven days after signing the contract to change your mind.

What about cooling-off periods for purchases over the internet?

You have the right to back out and cancel an internet purchase within seven days.

Are verbal contracts binding?

In Scotland a verbal contract is binding as long as the whole terms of the deal are clearly agreed and can be proved (verbal evidence may be sufficient). However, for certain categories of agreement, documents are needed, such as for the sale of land and buildings, a lease for more than one year or for loans of money. For these there usually needs to be a formally signed document.

Can I return faulty goods?

If you buy goods that are of unsatisfactory quality, are not fit for the purpose intended or are not as described by the seller on the packaging from a commercial seller, you have the right to reject the goods and get your money back. If you find this out within six months of purchase, the onus is on the supplier to disprove your allegation of unfitness. The law provides remedies of repair, partial or full refund, depending on the circumstances and the wishes of the purchaser.

Can I return a second hand item, such as a car?

Yes, if it is sold to you by a commercial seller or dealer, and it is not of reasonable quality, especially if it has defects that were not readily visible or accessible to you when you first bought it, or there has been misrepresentation, say about mileage or previous damage to it.

What if the car dealer says that a repair is not covered by the warranty I purchased?

A purchased warranty is a contract, and both parties (buyer and seller) are bound by the precise terms of it, so some work or parts may not be included in the warranty. However, a warranty can only enhance, not limit, your statutory consumer rights. This means that if you have a right of repair or refund under the law, it does not matter what the additional contractual warranty says or does not say. Indeed, you should check what the warranty gives you before you spend money on it as it may not add anything to your automatic legal protections. Note also that a manufacturer's warranty is separate from the statutory protections given by law and again cannot erode it, but only enhance it.

Can I insist upon a refund for any returned goods or must I accept a credit note or a repair?

If you have a legal right to reject goods under the law, you don't need to take a credit note or a replacement item, but can insist on repayment of money.

Can I return all goods bought?

If goods are not faulty or unsatisfactory, you have no right to a refund. Many shops have a returns policy and will give you money back without asking any questions, but this is their commercial choice, not a legal requirement. Once you have bought the goods, the contract is complete and cannot be cancelled by you. So buying goods as a gift is risky, especially if you are guessing the size (or taste) of the person receiving them.

What if I no longer have a receipt?

You should obviously keep a receipt to prove a purchase, but if it has gone missing for any reason other evidence may be enough: for example, credit card transaction slips or statements, bank statements or your word may even be accepted.

Who is liable for reimbursing me for faulty goods: the retailer or manufacturer?

It is always the retailer who is legally liable to return your money. The fact that they did not make the goods and that they were packed up and could not be checked is irrelevant. Whatever remedy the retailer has against his supplier or the manufacturer is no concern of yours. The retailer cannot avoid this liability as it is enshrined in consumer law.

What happens when goods bought on credit are faulty?

Consumer rights apply in finance cases just the same as cash purchases. These are called debtor-creditor-supplier cases, and the credit provider has equal liability with the seller to refund you if the goods are not of satisfactory quality or if there is a relevant breach of your statutory consumer rights. In fact, if the retailer is sticky about refunding you, it may be wise to intimate the rejection of the goods direct to the credit card company who may be more willing to cancel the contract and avoid a potential court case.

How do I prove goods are of unsatisfactory quality? What if the retailer says I must have damaged the goods after purchase?

Often it is self-evident what is wrong with goods, but, in the event of a dispute, you can call in the Trading Standards Officer of the local authority to get involved, or you can get an expert in the type of goods or equipment at issue to inspect and report. That report will either persuade the retailer, or, if necessary, be your evidence if you have to sue for damages and breach of contract. However, remember that the onus of proof for goods purchased less than six months before puts the onus on the seller to *disprove* the faults.

What if the retailer fails to co-operate or denies liability?

He is in breach of contract and his statutory duties and you can take him to court. First, though, you should report him to the local Trading Standards Office, and get a solicitor to write a threatening letter to see if a bit of legal and official pressure can shift him. A court action is slow, potentially expensive and can be unpleasant.

Can I get legal aid for a consumer dispute?

If you are eligible on financial means, legal advice and assistance is available. If you have to take the case to court, then civil legal aid may be available, unless the value at issue is less than £750, in which case the matter will go to the small claims court, where there is no legal aid. See chapter 15 on Civil Law and Procedure.

What public or local authority bodies can I refer a dispute or problem to?

For purchases that have gone wrong you can consult a solicitor, take advice from the CAB or speak to the Trading Standards Office of your local authority. The Trading Standards Office can investigate a complaint and bring pressure to bear on traders who fail their customers.

Services

What if I hire a company to do work or provide a service and they keep delaying completion or performance?

You are best to specify, in writing preferably, a fixed date for completion or a cut-off date, so this becomes a condition of the contract. Failure of the contractor to meet the date means that he is in breach of contract and can be sued, or the contract can be terminated and given to someone else, and allowing you damages for any losses you sustain. However, even if not so specified, the law assumes that jobs will be done in a reasonable period of time for that type of trade. For example, there was a case in which a customer put his car in for a repair and the garage kept it for eight weeks. He sued the garage for the cost of a hired car for three weeks. The court accepted that the job should not have taken any more than five weeks, so awarded him some hire costs.

If I hire a firm to do work on my house which is unsatisfactory, can I refuse to pay? What if I have paid in advance?

As ever, prevention is better than cure. There is no law that requires you to pay for services in advance. A company may say that this is their insistence, but at very least you have the option not to do business with them but to try other firms. Once you have paid up, you are at their mercy. If you have paid in advance, then failure of the contractor to complete the job or to carry it out in a competent professional or commercial manner puts them in breach of contract. You have two main legal remedies, assuming a polite letter to the managing director falls on deaf and well-paid ears. The two remedies are: getting the job done or re-done by another firm and suing the original firm for the additional costs you have incurred; or suing the original firm by way of an action of specific implement of the contract (that is getting a court order forcing them to do or complete the work) failing which, damages.

What if the contractor says the work has been done properly and demands payment?

To take court action against a tradesman or company requires some preparation. Before you sue, or are sued, you should get professional evidence of the bad workmanship of the firm. This evidence can be obtained by getting in another professional contractor to examine and report on whatever work you are complaining of (you should also gather your own evidence by taking photos, making notes and, where possible, recording conversations). Thus when the case comes to court and the original work has been obliterated by repairs or completion, there will be sufficient and reliable testimony to allow the court to understand the problem clearly.

What if a contractor says that as I am refusing to pay for work, he will remove his materials from my house?

This is a relatively common threat, but is almost always ineffective if the contractor has not done the work properly. It is a not unusual term of a contract with a firm doing work in your home that, until payment of the price of the work is made in full, the firm retains title to all materials. This is perfectly sound as a legal clause. However, the contractor has no right to enter your property without your consent, and, without the ability to cross your threshold, he has no way of getting his materials back. His only remedy is to sue you, and you would defend the case on the grounds that the work was not done properly.

What if I put goods in for repair or storage and they are lost or damaged?

Whoever takes your property, to hold or work on it, has a duty of care towards it. If a watchmaker loses a watch in for overhaul then he is liable to the customer-owner to replace the value.

Is this the same situation as when I put my car into a private car park?

Not necessarily. If the car park operator advertises that the premises are secure and contracts with you on that basis, then you have a right to safety and good order of your vehicle. Where you are simply offered an unsecure parking bay, however, the operator is not guaranteeing security, but simply the legal right to leave your car there. Security is not implied just because you pay for parking your car on someone else's property.

Banking

What do I do if my bank has made a mistake or I think they have charged me too much?

When you open a bank account, it is a contract. The bank is bound to carry out its service with reasonable skill and care. If you think that it has broken the contract or made a negligent mistake, you can enforce your rights. First contact the person responsible or the bank manager. Do this in person, in writing, or by telephone. Keep notes of names of people you spoke to, and when. It is best to follow up a phone call with a letter, fax or email. If the problem can't be resolved, ask for details of the bank's formal complaints procedure. If the dispute cannot be settled within the bank, you will be sent a letter of deadlock. This is a final response letter from the bank. You can then take your complaint to the Banking Ombudsman, who provides a free service. You must do this within six months of receiving the letter of deadlock. He can order the bank to put things right and, if necessary, award financial compensation. The amount received is limited to the amount actually lost. Going to court should be a last resort as it is a lengthier and more costly process, and should only be explored if the Ombudsman cannot settle the dispute. In order to avoid further mistakes and problems you can of course change banks.

How do I know if my bank is entitled to impose charges on me, and what if I did not authorise the charges?

Your bank can impose charges on you either if they are mentioned in the original forms you signed opening up the account, or if you breach the contract entered into for the account. For example, you may write a cheque that will take the balance of your account beyond the agreed limit. To make yourself aware of any powers that the bank can use, read the small print on the account opening form, which describes your contract with the bank. Your signature on this form is authorisation for any charges that the bank imposes. Many people sign forms without reading the terms and conditions. Failing to read or know the conditions does not mean that you are not bound by the rules. Different banks have different charges, and some do not charge for services where others may do so. For example, some banks offer a 'cushion', where you will not be charged for accidentally overdrawing your account within a certain limit. Banks should also conform to the Banking Code, which is a list of strong guidelines issued by the Banking Code Standards Board, and which requires that banks advise you of the amount of charges that will be debited to your account 14 days in advance. Each bank is also expected to publish a list of transaction charges for general banking services. You can ask your local branch for a list of these at any time. If you do not have sufficient funds in the bank to cover the charge, the bank can take further action against you.

Insurance

I took out an insurance policy, but when I claimed on it I was turned down because the insurance company says that I am not covered. Can they do this?

Insurance of all sorts is a contract between you and the insurance companies, but it has special rules which ordinary contracts do not have. One fundamental duty on anyone entering an insurance policy/contract is that it is entered with the utmost good faith. This is shorthand for absolutely full disclosure of all matters asked by the insurer. In a life assurance or endowment policy, your health will be a crucial issue. If you are dying from chronic heart disease, then the insurer is entitled to know this before accepting the risk of insuring your life. If you take out a policy for permanent health cover, it is important to know if you have ever before been off work for health reasons. If you are getting car insurance, have you ever been in a crash before? If you are getting house insurance, have you ever been refused before by an insurer? Have you any previous convictions for criminal offences? As well as there being good commercial reasons for insurers to ask these questions, the law allows them to cancel policies or refuse claims if it turns out that you did something or have something which you did not disclose when you commenced the policy, or which you did not give a correct or truthful answer to when completing a questionnaire or application form. If you are turned down in error, you can sue the insurer for breach of contract and report them to the Financial Ombudsman.

Travel

What happens legally when I book a holiday?

When you book a holiday, a legally binding contract is made between you and the company providing the accommodation, package, flights or other transport arrangements. You have a right to expect the holiday that you booked and paid for. If you book a package, your contract will probably be with the tour operator, not the travel agent, and therefore any claim for losses would be against the tour operator. You can, however, sue your travel agent if they do not fulfil their job properly. The tour operator has comprehensive responsibility, and must have financial security to cover your costs.

How do I know a travel company is properly secure and bonded before booking my holiday?

Travel companies should be licensed. ATOL is the government-backed Air Travel Organiser's Licence. If you book in the United Kingdom a charter or discount scheduled flight, the company selling the seat must hold an ATOL licence. If your tour operator goes bust while you are on holiday, this fund ensures that you can finish your holiday and be flown home. This also covers some flight-only deals. The Association of British Travel Agents (ABTA) is a trade body of travel agents and tour operators. All members have to lodge a bond to protect the money that customers pay for their holidays. If the tour operator or travel agent goes bust while you are away, you will be brought home at no extra charge. If you have not yet travelled, you will receive a full refund. If something goes wrong with your holiday, you can use the ABTA arbitration scheme to obtain compensation adjudicated by an independent arbiter. This might be necessary if the brochure promises that the hotel has a swimming pool, but you arrive to discover that there is not one. The arbitration scheme is a low-cost alternative to court action. Whatever company you use for your holiday, find out if they are bonded, and get a copy of the conditions of the bond or statement of travellers' rights.

What can I do if something goes wrong while I am on holiday?

Be prepared in advance: take copies of your holiday booking form, the brochure and relevant telephone numbers. If there is an incident or your holiday does not fulfil expectations, ensure that you do the following:

- stay calm;
- take notes of everything that happens and everyone that you deal with;
- try to take names and contact details of everyone who helps or hinders you;
- take photographs or videos of any evidence;

- try to find witnesses to the problem and to all conversations with managers, representatives and couriers; and

- . . . stay calm.

Following these steps will mean that your claim or suit will be far easier to handle when you return home. Deliver the above information to your solicitor as soon as possible.

Will I be entitled to compensation if something goes wrong?

If you have suffered a loss as a result of a breach of your holiday contract, you will be entitled to compensation (damages). Financial awards will be made in respect of loss of value, loss of enjoyment and out-of-pocket expenses. You will almost never get the total cost of your holiday back. The law imposes upon you a duty to minimise your financial loss, and make the most of things while on holiday. Therefore, if you refuse to be moved from substandard rooms in one hotel to another hotel, your compensation will be reduced.

What happens if I book my flights and accommodation separately?

A non-package holiday may seem to be cost-effective. However, if there is a problem with the hotel, your claim or suit will be against it rather than a British tour operator. You would therefore have to raise proceedings abroad. Under the ATOL scheme, there is no automatic protection if you book direct with the airline. If you are in dispute with an airline, it is legally obliged to compensate you for distress or inconvenience. There is a financial limit to the amount recoverable for lost baggage. If you are bumped off a flight because an airline has deliberately overbooked the plane, you should be offered on-the-spot cash compensation; a free telephone call to your destination; meals during your wait; and overnight accommodation if necessary.

Chapter 9

Licences and Licensing

A LAFFERTY

Which official licences are needed for what activities?

There are few activities that are not controlled in some way by the state, either directly by national government institutions, or through local authority licensing bodies. It would take several books to give even a rough guide to them all, but below is a list of some of the common activities that require licences, and the bodies that are the relevant licensing authorities.

Activity	Licensing authority
Accountancy practice	Institute of Chartered Accountants in Scotland
Sale of alcohol	Local Authority Licensing Board
Amusement machines and gaming	Local Authority Licensing Board

Activity	Licensing authority
Keeping dangerous wild animals	Local Authority Licensing Board
Running a caravan site	Local Authority (Environmental Health Department)
Car boot sale	Local Authority Licensing Board
Care homes and other residential services	Care Commission
Childminding and children's nurseries	Care Commission
Consumer credit businesses	Office of Fair Trading
Debt collection	Office of Fair Trading
Dentistry practice	General Dental Council
Driving motor vehicles	Driver Vehicle Licensing Agency
Driving instructors	Driving Standards Agency
Entertainment, public	Local Authority Licensing Board
Explosives and fireworks: manufacturing, storing and keeping	Health and Safety Executive or Local Authority Licensing Board
Firearms and ammunition	Firearms Certificate from local Chief Officer of Police
Foster homes	Local Authority Social Work Department
Hunting and selling game	Game Licence
Hypnotism	Local Authority Licensing Board
Kennels: cats and dogs (and breeding)	Local Authority Licensing Board
Legal practice	Law Society of Scotland
Limited companies	Companies Registration Office
Market trading	Local Authority Licensing Board

Activity	Licensing authority
Marriage	Registrar, local Register Office
Medical practice	General Medical Council
Nursing practice	Nursing and Midwifery Council
Pet shops	Local Authority Environmental Health Department
Taxis	Local Authority Licensing Board
Waste disposal	Scottish Environmental Protection Agency

Chapter 10

Compensation Claims: Accidents and Illness

A. LAFFERTY

Can I claim for any accident that happens to me?

Not all accidents give rise to a claim. Our law is a fault-based system, so to obtain civil damages you must prove that some person or organisation which has a legal duty to you failed to carry out that duty, and that their failure led to or caused otherwise avoidable harm to come to you. The onus is on you as the claimant/pursuer to prove this lack of care or breach of duty. If you contributed to the accident by your own carelessness, then this is contributory negligence and may reduce your award, even to nil in some cases.

What kinds of accident or illness cases are there?

The main ones are:

- **Accidents at work:** where you sustain injury or illness as a result of, for example, using faulty equipment at work; an employer or co-worker's negligence; an unsafe system of work; or health and safety or other requirements being broken. All employers have a duty to provide a reasonably safe environment, and they are responsible (by vicarious liability) for the actions of their other employees as they affect you.

- **Road traffic accidents:** where you are a driver, passenger or pedestrian and are injured by a driver who drove carelessly or dangerously.

- **Accidents in public places:** where you are injured in a public place, such as a shop, an office building or a football stadium. Anywhere the public have a right to be, the occupier is liable for the safety of users – examples include: where yoghurt has spilled on a supermarket floor; a signboard falling off the frontage of a hotel; or the lights going out as you descend a stair at the bank.

- **Accidents on the street or pavement:** where you trip, slip or fall and suffer injury and loss due to the disrepair of a publicly maintained street. The local or other authority with the duty of maintaining and repairing the street is liable if they failed in their duty.

- **Product liability:** where you become ill from food or drink products, if a car's brakes fail and cause a crash, or a toaster electrocutes you.

- **Sports injuries:** usually a rough sport like rugby or karate carries with it the chance of injury; however, if the rules are followed there may still be a claim. If there is deliberate violence by one player you may have a claim against the player who committed the aggression. Also, if there is negligence on the part of an official, such as a referee, that leads to or contributes to an accident, he or his governing body may be liable for damages. Note that sports bodies and clubs ought to be heavily insured for this very purpose.

What is a time bar and how long is it after the accident or illness before it comes in?

A time bar is a fatal obstruction to pursuing a claim for compensation. If you do not get financial settlement before the end of the three years, then you have to at least start a court action, or your claim will fall permanently by time bar. Broadly, this is three years after an incident causing physical harm, or after it came reasonably to your attention that you may have a condition that would cause a claim to be made. For professional negligence not involving physical harm or breach of contract cases, the period is five years.

What evidence is needed to prove negligence?

Evidence can be from eye or personal witnesses; medical personnel who treated you or have been asked for expert opinion (this can include a GP and/or specialists in the appropriate field of medical expertise); documentation; and/or research material. Evidence can be anything that will help your lawyers to show that the accident was the fault of the opponent and that their conduct did not meet the standard required of them by the law.

What evidence is needed to prove financial loss?

This is usually down to paperwork, including written confirmation from employers as to wages lost if an accident causes time off work; expenses incurred in additional transport such as taxis to clinics; pharmacy costs for prescriptions; equipment for medical or other treatment; or fees due for specialist reports on loss of employability or suitable re-employment.

How is compensation calculated?

Compensation (properly called damages) is based on the loss and injury you have suffered, not on the culpability of the person who caused the injury or disease. We do not, unlike some other legal systems, have a system of punitive or exemplary damages. For example, where two cars hit two pedestrians and one victim receives multiple fractures and is off work for months, but the other merely gets a bruised shin; the drivers were equally careless yet the first claimant would get tens of thousands, but the other, only a few hundred, pounds.

What categories of compensation are there?

Compensation is under a number of headings. The main ones are:

- **Solatium:** (called general damages in England) for pain and suffering. While logically it is nonsense to say that a broken wrist is worth one amount, an amputated arm worth another and post-traumatic stress disorder is worth yet another, the law has built up a price list for all sorts of diseases and injuries. These can also be increased or reduced by additional factors, such as the age and health or physical condition of the victim. Courts are bound by decisions of previous courts in cases involving similar injuries. There are now volumes of case reports which can be checked by courts, solicitors and insurance companies to compare and value claims.

- **Loss of earnings:** if you are off work because of an injury caused through the fault of someone else, then it is fair that that person or their insurers pay you back wages you have lost. If by the time the claim is settled or the court decides on an award you are still off work, then compensation for future loss of earnings is assessed. This is done with the assistance of medical evidence of the prognosis of your recovery in the future, as well as specialist evidence from an employment consultant if, for example, you cannot return to your previous employment and must look for new and less well-paid work.

- **Out-of-pocket expenses:** these may include necessary taxi fares to clinics for treatment; hire of a vehicle while yours is off the road; replacement of lost or damaged property, and many other examples.

- **Services:** if you have been injured and require either professional care, or additional care provided by a family member, or both, this can be calculated financially and claimed from the opponent.

- **Loss of society:** for a close family member whose (mainly) parent, child or spouse has been killed in an accident. There are well-accepted scales for compensation when a loved one has died. This is, however, an unsatisfactory area of damages, as the awards are pitiful when you consider the hurt of losing a child or a parent.

- **Loss of support:** if a person who dies in an accident provided the means of support for the family. For example, this could include a husband whose earnings were relied upon by a claimant widow and children.

- **Legal expenses:** to compensate you for the legal costs incurred in claiming compensation.

How do I know if I am getting a good settlement?

You have to trust your legal team and try not to listen to lay people who read in the paper last week that a worker who staved his toe received a quarter of a million pounds in compensation. Ask your solicitor to show you the legal basis of the award or settlement by reference to the decided court cases he or she is using as a guide to yours. The award or settlement should be based on comparisons with other decided and recorded court cases in Scotland and England.

How long does it take to settle a claim out of court?

If it is not settled within three years, your lawyers must get the case into court or it will be time barred permanently. However, there is no rule about how long a claim takes to settle. The more complex the case, the longer it will take to settle.

How long does it take to win a case in court?

Once a case is in court, it will take usually at least months and often years to be completed, even when your lawyers are doing everything as quickly as they can. Courts are not known for speed.

How much does it cost in legal fees for compensation cases?

If a case is settled out of court, there is a practice that an insurance company working for the person against whom you are claiming will pay a set fee to your lawyer, as well as the outlays for such items as medical report fees that you have incurred. However, this may not cover all your costs, in which case an agreed part of your award will be taken towards the balance of costs. This should be worked out in advance before you accept a settlement, so you know exactly what you are getting. If your lawyer is working on a speculative basis (sometimes known as 'no win, no fee') then he may be entitled to a higher fee than he would if he had simply been charging you for work done as the case went along. This is different to the United States of America where lawyers take a percentage of damages received. Your solicitor should make you aware of the basis of the fees charged at the outset of the case. If a case has to go to court instead of being settled out of court, and assuming you win or get a settlement before the end of the court case, fees may be charged differently. You may not get the insurance company to pay for fees and costs incurred before the commencement of the court part of the case. As to the court costs themselves, the loser usually pays the winner's costs. The exceptions to this are if the case settles before the end, in which case it is up to the parties to agree what is to happen to costs, or if you as the pursuer are on civil legal aid, in which case if you lose, your costs are normally nil. If you win, the opponents should pay them.

What is 'beating the tender'?

If you are suing for damages the defender/insurance company can put in a 'minute of tender', this is a written statement that they are prepared to pay you a set sum in damages. If you do not accept the minute of tender, then if at the end of the case the sheriff or judge awards you no more than that figure, you will be liable for all the costs incurred from the date of the tender onwards, on the basis that such work has been caused by you seeking an unrealistic or excessive figure. Note the judge does not see the amount in the minute of tender as the court copy of the minute is sealed and closed until the end of the case.

Is legal aid available for damages cases?

Yes, both Advice and Assistance, and civil legal aid, as long as you meet the personal financial criteria of income and capital. Your solicitor can assess you for this. However, if an award is made or settlement received, the Scottish Legal Aid Board has first call on the money to pay the legal fees incurred. This has always been a fundamental rule of legal aid, and solicitors in settling a claim must make sure as far as possible that an insurer pays the legal costs, or the bulk of them, over and above the compensation. Or if the settlement is a global one, the solicitor must make you aware (before you accept) of how much is to be deducted from your award to give a net figure to you.

If my claim goes to court, who decides on my award: a judge or a jury?

In the vast majority of civil cases the matter is decided by a single sheriff or judge. In some very large or special cases there is a right in the Court of Session to have a civil jury which decides on the issues of liability and the amount of damages to be awarded.

Do I get the whole of my award or are there deductions?

If as a result of the accident or illness you have received state benefits of certain sorts which you would not have been entitled to if you had not had the accident, then the Benefits Agency have a right to claw them back. Under the present system the Compensation Recovery Unit (CRU) of the Benefits Agency claws back these benefits from the insurance company which pays the compensation, but they are deducted from part of your award, and so in effect you pay them. You instinctively think of this as a reduction of your full compensation, but logically you are only paying back what you have got extra in benefits. If you got no recoverable benefits, there is no deduction from the award. Compensation Recovery, as it is properly called, is deducted only from the loss of earnings part of the award or settlement, not from the *solatium* element. Also, if your legal team have been working on a 'no win, no fee' basis, there may be a sum due to them out of your award, but not a percentage as in American civil practice.

Can I get interim payments during a claim?

Yes, although this is usually only in cases where liability is already admitted by the insurer and a settlement is therefore in effect guaranteed. There are no rules about interim payments; it is up to your side and the opposition to negotiate based on what you urgently need. This is a double-edged sword, as the more interim award you get, the less you will necessarily get at the end of the case. Remember that compensation once paid cannot be revisited; it is in full and final settlement for all losses present and future, so you cannot go back later and ask for more after a final award. Thinking of the long term is the best policy.

How do I get criminal injuries compensation?

If you have been the victim of a crime then you may be entitled to financial compensation from the Criminal Injuries Compensation Authority. You can get the application form from a solicitor, a Citizens' Advice Bureau, or from the Authority itself. You complete and submit the form and the Authority investigates the case and decides what, if any, award to make. If you are dissatisfied with the amount of the award, or if you are refused completely, you may appeal and attend a hearing to present your reasons for the appeal to a panel of the Authority presided over by a Queen's Counsel (you can be legally represented but legal aid is not available). Reasons for refusing an award include: where the victim provoked the attack through drunken or aggressive behaviour; being a willing participant in a fight; or having previous criminal convictions yourself. The essence of a successful claim is that you are a genuinely innocent victim of a deliberate act of violence. There are special rules where the attack is by a family member with whom you are or were living. In almost every case you must make the application no later than two years after the event complained of, or else your right is lost by time bar. The compensation is on a strict tariff system which you can check in a booklet available from the Criminal Injuries Compensation Authority.

What if I am injured by an uninsured car driver?

Drivers are of course required to be insured at all times so that injury and damage caused to third parties will always be paid for. It is an offence to drive without insurance in place; however, it does happen. The insurance industry has an agreement that victims of uninsured drivers are compensated by the Motor Insurers Bureau, which in effect steps in as a 'legal' insurer, and processes a claim in the normal way. It reserves the right to seek repayment of any outlay it makes from the uninsured driver, but the victim of the driver does not need to be concerned with this, as they receive settlement directly from the Motor Insurers Bureau.

Do I need an independent witness to prove the other driver was at fault?

No. If there is clear enough evidence from one source of the negligence of the other driver, that can be sufficient (in the criminal law, but not civil claims, corroboration is always required). Remember that even if there is only one eye-witness, there will often be physical or circumstantial evidence: for example, the other driver was breathalysed and found positive; skid marks on the road lead from his side to yours; or his car's brakes were found to be defective.

How do I go about starting a claim for personal injuries, and what happens?

If you are a driver, you should report the accident to your insurer, even if it was not your fault. The insurer may want to negotiate with the other insurance company, though this will be about the damage to vehicles. You should consult a solicitor and provide him or her with all the information and evidence that you have about the accident. The solicitor will intimate by letter a claim for damages against the other driver, and tell him to pass the matter on to his insurers or lawyers. It is usual for the other driver's insurers to carry out their own investigation, and let your lawyer know if they admit liability or not. Your lawyer in the meantime will be collecting evidence from witnesses, getting a police accident report, obtaining medical evidence of your injuries and information on any losses, such as lost earnings, that you have suffered. He will assess the claim and work out the appropriate compensation due. If the insurance company admits liability (that is, agrees that their client was to blame) then they will proceed to negotiate the amounts of compensation with your solicitor. If agreement can be reached between you and the insurer, settlement will take place and you will receive payment. If no acceptable offer is made after all, then your choices are to accept the offer anyway, or to proceed to raise a court action against the other driver, leaving it up to a judge or sheriff to award compensation.

Although this is a fairly lengthy answer, it is no more than a thumbnail sketch of a claim process. Claims can take months or years, and can go through many slow and tortuous stages. Insurance companies try to make them go even more slowly than they ought. You will need to be patient. For other kinds of accident or illness, at work or as a result of medical negligence, the same principles of gathering evidence and taking legal advice apply.

What if the insurance company says I was to blame for the accident?

The previous answer can apply to you in reverse; you may be the 'other driver' and your insurer may have to negotiate the claim on your behalf. If you are the claimant, however, and the other party's insurer defends its customer by saying the accident was not his fault, but either partly or totally yours, then this can cause a range of results. If you deny any part of blame, then you would have to resolve the question of liability at court on the evidence. If you are right, then you will get decree in your favour. If you are found to be wrong, you will lose your case. However, if you admit or are found to be partly to blame, your award will be reduced by a percentage appropriate to your share of the liability. This is known as contributory negligence, and can strike out a percentage of the claim from 1% to 100% depending on the share of blame you have for the accident. Note that the principles of contributory negligence can apply to you as the claimant *or* pursuer.

If I am the victim of a crash, can I hire a car while my own is off the road being repaired?

Yes you can, although, if liability is in dispute with the insurer, you may have to pay the cost of this and claim it back as part of the overall compensation. If liability is admitted, it is usually possible to get an interim payment from the insurer to cover essential or urgent costs. You must hire a suitable and appropriate car; if your car is a Fiesta, you cannot hire a Rolls Royce.

Do I need to be represented by the lawyer chosen for me by my insurance company?

No, but you would be responsible for agreeing fees with your own choice of lawyer beforehand, whereas if it is your insurer's chosen lawyer, the fees are normally taken care of by the insurer.

What happens if the accident takes place offshore or abroad?

If you are injured while on holiday abroad, you may have a claim against a package tour operator. If you booked flights and accommodation separately, you will have to sue the person or company responsible abroad in the foreign courts. If you are working for a company abroad that is based in the United Kingdom, the general rule is that your claim would take place in the courts of the country where the accident occurred. However, this rule can be overcome if there are significant factors which connect the injury to a different country from that. The domicile or place of business of the employer would help to decide which country is more appropriate to go to court in. Therefore, it is likely that a United Kingdom employer would be sued in the United Kingdom courts. If the company has a registered place of business in the United States, it may be profitable to try and sue there in light of the higher compensation awards. Foreign territorial waters are regarded as part of the country to which they belong. If you are to sue abroad, it is important to bear in mind that different jurisdictions have different laws, time bars and procedural rules.

Chapter 11

Employment

Please note: Employment law is meant to be based on common sense and fairness, to balance the rights of employers and employees. The reality is that it has become a complex and detailed collection of statutes, regulations, codes of practice and procedures. It is an area of law where professional representation is, in my experience, crucial.

In the workplace, what are my rights?

As an employee you have a wide range of detailed rights, but here are the basic ones:

- the right to remuneration (salary or wages);
- the right to fair and equal treatment;
- the right to working conditions that comply with health and safety regulations;
- the right to have expenses reimbursed if they are incurred while carrying out duties; and
- the right to a complaints procedure for grievances.

In return, you owe duties to your employer, including being able and willing to work, conducting yourself properly, obeying reasonable orders and demonstrating fidelity, which includes confidentiality and promoting your employer's interests.

Do I have job security, or can I be sacked without reason?

If your contract of employment gives you protection from being fired without reason, then you can rely on that. If not, then after you have been with the same employer for at least one year continuously, you cannot be sacked unfairly. Until then you can be sacked for any or no reason (although note that there is no minimum qualifying period for dismissal on some grounds, including legitimate union activity, sex, disability or racial discrimination). Once you have security, you can apply to an employment (industrial) tribunal to seek compensation, reinstatement or re-engagement (in a different job with the same employer).

Do I have the right to notice if dismissed?

If you have been guilty of gross misconduct then you can be dismissed summarily; however, if your employer did not consider your case thoroughly or make a fair decision after following fair procedure, the dismissal may still be unfair. If you have worked at least one month for an employer, you are entitled to one week's notice of dismissal, and thereafter an additional one week per year up to a maximum of 12 weeks' notice. Your contract may give a longer period of notice entitlement, though not a shorter one. Do not be confused between notice, which is administrative, and the fairness of dismissal, which goes to whether the dismissal should have taken place at all.

On what grounds can an employer sack me if I have security?

Dismissal will only be fair if it is for one of the following reasons:

- you are incapable of doing the work;
- you have been guilty of misconduct;
- there has been a fair selection for redundancy;
- it is legally impossible for you to continue your job (for example, you are a driver and get banned from driving); or
- there is 'some other substantial reason' to justify dismissal.

A 'substantial reason' can be if you work in a trusted capacity with money and you have been caught shoplifting or you are a youth worker who has been convicted of child abuse.

If I am sacked or made redundant, how can I get compensation or my job back?

If your dismissal is unfair, you can apply to the Employment Tribunal for an order making the employer pay compensation to you or give you your job back or another one. You can get the forms from your solicitor, the Advisory, Conciliation and Arbitration Service (ACAS), the Citizens' Advice Bureau (CAB), your nearest Employment Tribunal office or the Central Office of Employment Tribunals. The form you need is called IT1 (note that the abbreviation was not changed when Industrial Tribunals became Employment Tribunals). The form should be completed (either by you or with professional help) and submitted to the tribunal. The form contains space for information from you on yourself; your employer; the dates of commencement and conclusion of employment; whether you want compensation, reinstatement or re-engagement; and an explanation of the basis of your case. This form must be lodged within three months of the effective date of termination of your employment. If you are late, your case will be time barred unless there is a special reason for its lateness. The tribunal will then ask the employer to reply and will then fix a hearing of the case. There may be legal or other preliminary matters to deal with before that. Employers almost always have lawyers representing them. If you do not have a lawyer you can represent yourself, and the tribunal is duty-bound to make sure you have a fair hearing. If possible, however, you should have a representative with you, either a lawyer or another experienced person. Legal aid is available in some circumstances (see chapter 21 on legal aid). At the full hearing, evidence and legal arguments are presented by both sides, and the tribunal makes its decision as to: (a) whether you were unfairly dismissed; and (b) if so, how much, if any, compensation you are due. Any orders the Employment Tribunal makes can be legally enforced like a court order.

What orders can the Employment Tribunal make?

The tribunal can make the following three main orders:

- **Reinstatement:** ordering the employer to treat you as though the dismissal did not occur, so you are entitled to return to the same job with the same terms and conditions.

- **Re-engagement:** where you are re-employed by the employer, but it may not be in the same job, and there may be different terms and conditions.

- **Compensation**: awards made for loss of earnings and expenses reasonably incurred. This is the most common remedy which may also accompany one of the above. This award is calculated principally according to your time employed, wages lost both before, and sometimes after, the tribunal date and difficulties in obtaining alternative employment.

In making a reinstatement or re-engagement order, the tribunal is obliged to consider your wishes, the practicality of the decision and whether it would be fair to make the order. The tribunal can also make a range of incidental orders or preliminary findings: for example, that an applicant was of employed status, if this is being contested by the employer (on the basis that some workers are self-employed contractors rather than employees, and thus do not enjoy legal protection against unfair dismissal), and the issue requires to be determined before the merits of the case can be heard later. There are a great many such procedural or preliminary matters in current employment law.

How can Employment Tribunal orders be enforced if employers ignore them?

Just as with a court order, if an employer does not comply with the decision of the tribunal, the matter can be placed in the hands of sheriff officers. They can carry out the arrestment of bank accounts, attachment and sale of company property, or a firm or company can be threatened with winding up/liquidation to ensure orders are complied with. However, if an employer is liquidated, or for that matter has no assets or money, such enforcement action may not be effective! Nevertheless, orders by tribunals are generally complied with, simply because they are legally binding.

What will it cost me to go to an Employment Tribunal?

Unlike in the civil courts, there is no booking fee when you make an application to the tribunal. If you win or lose the case, then you will almost certainly not either be found liable for a successful opponent's costs, or have an unsuccessful opponent liable for your costs. If you hire a lawyer and are not eligible for legal aid, you should be able to get at least a rough approximation of the costs from your lawyer before proceeding with the case. There are some schemes for free representation in tribunal cases, but a solicitor is likely to cost you several hundreds of pounds at the least, and into four figures if it is a complex case, or one with a lot of evidence or witnesses.

Is there legal aid for Employment Tribunal cases?

For those who qualify financially there is always Advice and Assistance to allow your lawyer to carry out preliminary or preparatory work for a tribunal case. For the conduct of the hearing(s) at the tribunal, there is a special form of legal aid called Advice by Way of Representation (ABWOR) which can be granted to pay your legal costs, again if you qualify financially, and if the Scottish Legal Aid Board considers that it is right to award it. It is not automatic and you may have to pay a contribution.

What if I am unhappy with the Employment Tribunal award or decision refusing compensation?

Within 42 days of getting the decision of the tribunal in writing you must appeal (in writing and in proper form) to the Employment Appeal Tribunal in Edinburgh. This is a superior tribunal presided over by a Court of Session judge, and will adjudicate on points of law wrongly decided by the original tribunal. It will not usually overrule the tribunal on the facts or evidence. It can order the tribunal to reconsider its decision, order a re-hearing and even send the case to a different tribunal to re-hear the case or part of it. If you are unhappy with the Employment Appeal Tribunal's decision, it is possible to appeal points of law to the Court of Session, then to the House of Lords and finally to the European Court. The costs for these appeals are heavy, and legal aid is available on the usual basis. Either side can appeal against a ruling.

Am I entitled to a written contract of employment?

After two months from starting work, the employer must give you a written statement containing:

- the names of the employer and employee;
- the start date;
- the date on which continuous employment began if this includes service with a previous employer for the job;
- the rate or scale of remuneration;
- the intervals at which remuneration is paid;
- the terms and conditions relating to hours of work;
- holiday entitlement, pensions, and incapacity and sick pay provisions;
- length of notice to be given;
- job title;
- period of employment (permanent or the length of a fixed-term contract);
- the place of work;
- any collective agreement; and
- any provisions as to working overseas.

If the employer does not provide this or the written statement is incomplete, and a request or demand by you for the statement is ignored, you can apply to a tribunal to decide what should be in it. Note that you are also entitled to an itemised pay statement.

Which holidays am I entitled to?

Again, your contract of employment may state this, but under the Working Time Regulations 1998, all workers are entitled to four weeks' paid holiday per year. There is no legal right to public or bank holidays on top of these four weeks. For working part of a year, you are entitled to 1/12 of the annual entitlement for every month worked.

Do I have to work on Sundays?

Recent legislation protects workers in shops or betting premises. From April 2004, workers will no longer have to work on Sundays. If your initial contract of employment does not include a requirement to work on Sundays, you cannot be forced to do so by the employer. You can, however, give an *opting-in notice* which would alter your contract and give an express agreement to work on Sundays. If your contract says that you may be required to work on Sundays, you can give an *opting-out notice* which gives the employer three months' notice that you object to Sunday work. You will be protected from dismissal and redundancy. The law does not apply to you if you have been employed only to work on Sundays.

Can an employer make deductions from my wages?

Unless you have agreed in writing, or it is in your original contract of employment or another document that an employer can deduct from your wages in respect of shortages, debts or the like, then they have no power to do so. In any event the employer must be able to show that the deduction is justified, and was not retrospective to the employee giving consent. There are exceptions to this rule, however; if wages or expenses are mistakenly overpaid or fraudulently claimed, the employer can deduct from the employee's wages to balance up. The same applies if there is money due to a public authority, if the employee has been on strike, or if a court has made an order in favour of the employer for payment by the employee. There is also a very specific situation for retail employees. Employers can take deductions for cash shortages or stock defaults from employees, but only if: (a) there is a contractual provision to this effect; and (b) the deductions do not exceed 10% of gross wages. If an unlawful deduction has been made, an employee can bring a complaint to the Employment Tribunal within three months of the deduction.

What is the minimum wage, and who qualifies?

The law requiring payment of minimum wage applies to all workers, but with some exceptions, amongst which are:

- workers under 18 and apprentices aged 16–26 in the first year of apprenticeship;
- trainee teachers;
- some special schemes for classes of workers defined, for example some apprentices between the ages of 19 and 25;
- au pairs, nannies and the like; and
- members of employers' families who live at home and help to run family businesses.

If you think you are being paid less than the law dictates, you can take the employer to court or to the Employment Tribunal, either as a claim under the Employment Rights Act 1996 for unlawful deduction, or for breach of contract. There are also government enforcement officers in the Inland Revenue who can require employers to act lawfully.

What if the employer wants to change my work/hours/ wages?

An employer must notify a change in terms or conditions within one month of the change. As to the enforceability of a change, look as ever to the contract of employment. It may give the right to employers to make alterations to work or wages. If it is silent, or there is no written contract, then any attempt to change things to the detriment of the employee is a breach of contract. This can lead to legally difficult choices. If the breach or change is so fundamental that the employee cannot be expected to accept it, he could resign and claim constructive dismissal, making it possible to get compensation from the tribunal. Alternatively the employee could stay in the job and sue the employer for the difference in wages.

A contract of employment may, however, lawfully be changed through external factors: for example, when it is financially necessary. An employee who refuses the change after consultation, and who is then sacked, may be fairly dismissed under the category of dismissal for 'some other substantial reason' as long as the employers act reasonably. For example, where there has been inevitable technological change in the workplace and a worker has refused offered training, or has been incapable of learning the new skills.

What is constructive dismissal?

Where an employer is in breach of contract, and the employee sees himself as having no alternative but to 'accept' that the breach has happened (that is, not to protest further over it while remaining in post) and leave, what appears to be a resignation is treated as if the employer dismissed the employee. A basic example of this would be if an employer stops paying the employee's wages but tells him to keep coming to work. In this situation the employer has not said 'you are sacked', but has made it impossible for the employee to continue working. Thus the employee has been constructively dismissed, and if that dismissal is unfair, and the employee has been in the post at least a year, he can make an application to the Employment Tribunal. To justify a tribunal application, the breach must be fundamental to the contract of employment. Examples are incredibly many and varied, but one might be where a person is a sales manager, and is told that he or she must achieve the same targets as before, but with only half the representatives working on the territory. When the case comes to a hearing, the onus is primarily on the employee to establish why his leaving was a constructive dismissal and not a resignation done hastily or unnecessarily. Resigning on the basis of constructive dismissal is a very risky step and should only be done with legal advice and in extreme circumstances.

What responsibility for health and safety does my employer have?

All employers have a basic duty to provide a safe system of work for staff, safe equipment, suitable premises and facilities. Any employer with five or more staff should have a written safety policy, and may not fairly dismiss employees who carry out safety activities, bring safety issues to the employer's attention, refuse to carry out unsafe procedures or take steps to protect himself or others from danger. An employee who reports an employer for bad practice and is sacked may go to the Employment Tribunal.

What if I suffer an injury from having defective equipment at work?

It is the legal duty of all controllers of work premises (owner-occupiers and tenants) to ensure, as far as reasonably practicable, that workstations, machinery, equipment and materials employed in the workplace are all safe. Also designers, manufacturers and suppliers of equipment have a duty to ensure it is safe and properly tested. There are numerous regulations to deal with specific situations and types of equipment and premises. If the employer or any other party breaches these regulations or requirements, there is usually a criminal penalty, and they can also be sued for civil damages by you as an employee.

How can an employer make me redundant?

You can be made redundant because your employer does not require or can no longer afford as many staff, or because he has gone bust. He cannot use the guise of redundancy to dismiss you for any other reason. The employer must undergo a process of consultation; this involves meeting with employees, employee representatives and any relevant trade union prior to enforced redundancies. If he fails to do this, or does not fulfil this obligation within set time limits, you may have a claim for unfair dismissal. Your employer must present the union with a written document containing the reasons for redundancies, numbers and descriptions of proposed employees, the method of selection of employees, the method for carrying out dismissals and the method for calculating redundancy payments. You may be entitled to a redundancy payment; however, if your employer offers you similar alternative employment within four weeks of redundancy, you will probably not receive a payment. In calculating payments, age and length of service are taken into account. You must have been employed by your employer for a period of at least two years before being made redundant (the minimum payment is one week's pay for every year worked). You must be at least 18 years old. Part-time employees qualify for payments on the same basis as full-time employees.

What if I want to whistle-blow on my employer for unsafe practice etc?

There is protection for employees who disclose information of wrongdoings at work. The disclosure must show that one of the following has occurred or is likely to occur: a criminal offence; a failure to comply with a legal obligation; a miscarriage of justice; health and safety dangers; environmental hazards; or the deliberate concealment of any of these. Your disclosure must be made in good faith, that is with the objective of improving the safety of employees or the public. The report should be made to the employer, legal adviser or a government official or agency. If you are victimised at work or dismissed as a result of whistle-blowing, you can make a complaint to an Employment Tribunal. You may be entitled to compensation.

How does discrimination affect employment and how do I know if I have suffered from discrimination?

Discrimination involves treating someone unfairly or differently because of their sex, sexual orientation, marital status, pregnancy, religion, race or disability. Employers are prohibited from discrimination against job applicants and employees in relation to recruitment, job offer terms, access to opportunities for promotion, transfer or training and access to benefits, facilities and services. Dismissal due to any of the above factors is also unlawful. Self-employed persons and those performing contracted services are also protected. Unlike ordinary unfair dismissal, there is no minimum qualifying period of service required for the right to challenge discrimination in a tribunal. In fact, a valid complaint may arise because a person feels that they have been discriminated against in the job application process.

What kinds of examples of sex discrimination are there?

There are two main categories of sex discrimination:

(1)   **Direct discrimination** involves treating one sex less favourably than the other is, or would be, treated. Adverse treatment on the grounds of pregnancy is an example of this, as only women can get pregnant. Cases of direct discrimination are usually easy to identify.

(2)   **Indirect discrimination** is where an employer imposes a condition that is more difficult for a member of one sex to meet. For example, a requirement that a job be performed on a full-time basis potentially discriminates against women because they are often less able to work full-time than men.

Discrimination can be justified, for example, if a male actor is required for a particular part in a play, or a female cleaner is required to work in a ladies' changing room. Positive discrimination for disabled persons or disadvantaged groups may be justified and legal, say to help the economic regeneration of a local community, or to rebalance an unfair employment situation in an area.

I am pregnant, what are my rights?

You have the right not to be dismissed from your place of employment for becoming pregnant. If you are no longer able to perform the job due to your pregnancy, your employer must find alternative work for you. If this is not possible, you can be suspended with pay. You can have time off work for antenatal care, but may have to provide your employer with proof of hospital appointments. You can take 26 weeks of maternity leave, with statutory pay. You must give 28 days' notice of when you intend to commence maternity leave, or notify your employer as soon as reasonably practicable. You also have the right to return to work after maternity leave, although you must give written notice of your intention to do so. The right to return relates to the job which you held before your maternity leave, and to the pay that you would be receiving had you not been absent at all. While absent, you must be treated as though your employment is continuing, apart from levels of pay. This means that your holiday entitlement will continue to accrue and you should still enjoy any benefits, such as a company car. Your contract of employment may offer you more rights than the above statutory requirements, but not less. Fathers (and mothers and anyone else with 'parental responsibility') who have one years' service with an employer are also entitled to two weeks' leave with statutory paternity pay and up to 13 weeks' unpaid leave. A prospective father must give notice to the employer of his intention to take it. The leave must be taken between the birth of the child and 56 days after the birth.

As a woman, am I entitled to equal pay with a man?

It is unlawful to offer different pay and conditions (pensions and perks etc) to men who are doing the same or equivalently rated work. Even where two posts look apparently dissimilar, the employer cannot offer unequal pay for work of equal value in terms of demands made under such headings as effort, skill and decision-making. The law does not permit claims for equal pay with other people of the same sex, or between different employers. Anyone who considers they have reason to complain can lodge a claim at an Employment Tribunal while they are still doing the job, or within six months of leaving it.

Is it unlawful for an employer to discriminate on the grounds of my sexual orientation?

Yes, as of 2003. Whether you are an employee or a contract worker, to treat you less favourably, to dismiss you, to fail or refuse to offer you a job, to deny you training, or to do anything that disadvantages you because of your sexual orientation is unlawful, and can be the basis of an application to the Employment Tribunal. Religious organisations are, however, exempted. Note that same-sex partners still do not have the same pension rights and benefits as married couples.

Is it unlawful for an employer to discriminate on the grounds of my race?

It is unlawful to discriminate against a person on the grounds of colour, race, nationality or ethnic origin. Direct discrimination arises if a person is treated less favourably as a result. It is not necessary for an employer to have a discriminatory motive. For example, if an employer segregates employees by nationality he discriminates, even if he believes that the employee would otherwise be subject to racial taunts. Indirect racial discrimination is where an employer imposes a condition where the proportion of persons from one racial group that can comply is smaller than the proportion of persons from other groups. Here an employer may be able to justify the condition if he can show that it was not imposed for discriminatory reasons. For example, if a company has legitimate hygiene rules that prevent the growing of beards, this would not amount to discrimination against Sikhs even though it would prevent them from working for the employer. An example of unlawful indirect discrimination is requiring job applicants to complete a form in English in their own handwriting, even though the job does not actually involve any writing.

Is it unlawful for an employer to discriminate on the grounds of my disability?

A person who has a physical or mental impairment that has a substantial long-term effect on their ability to carry out normal day-to-day activities is protected against discrimination. Discrimination occurs where there is unfavourable treatment for a reason that relates to a disabled person's disability. Direct and indirect disability discrimination can be justified. For example, an employer who requires a job applicant to have a driving licence because the job involves driving is not discriminating. In contrast, requiring applicants to have a driving licence to work in an office would be discrimination. An employer also has a duty to make reasonable adjustments for any disabled employees. This means that he may have to alter premises, work hours, place of work or provide supervision. This duty only exists if the disabled person is placed at a substantial disadvantage by the working conditions or the premises. An employer of a disabled person could still be discriminating against that person if he has not made reasonable adjustments, such as having ramps and suitable toilets. Some small businesses are exempt from some requirements of disability discrimination law if it would be unreasonable to have to put undue financial strain on a business for a limited benefit. Note that it would probably not be justified to create a special provision for disabled customers and then charge them more than other service users. It is worth noting that in this area positive discrimination is acceptable for disabled persons, but in relation to other groups, for training only.

Is it unlawful for an employer to discriminate on the grounds of my religion?

As of 2003, the law prohibits direct discrimination, indirect discrimination, victimisation and harassment on the grounds of religion, in areas such as recruitment, promotion, the terms and conditions of employment and dismissal. The term 'religion or belief' is defined as 'any religion, religious belief, or similar philosophical belief'. It does not include philosophical or political beliefs unless they are similar to a religious belief, so this excludes the likes of anti-abortion campaigners, even if they are basing their attitudes or actions on Christian or religious observance. While Christians, Muslims and Jews will clearly be covered, defining what constitutes a religion or a belief is a grey area. Are Druids, Pagans and Rastafarians included, for example? Some employment lawyers believe they are. The law does cover those who have no belief. The main exception is discrimination where there is a genuine occupational requirement that the holder of the job is of a particular religious belief. The job of a teacher in a religious school would most probably be considered a post where discrimination should be allowed. Churches and other organisations based on a religious or belief ethos may also be successful in stating a genuine occupational requirement. Note that if a religious organisation or a large group of its adherents genuinely believes that it would be contrary to its doctrine to hire someone of a specific sexual orientation, it can claim an exemption for the 2003 sexual orientation legislation.

What can I do if I have been discriminated against?

Consult your solicitor as soon as possible. When making applications to the Employment Tribunal, there are strict time limits. The rules of proof vary for different types of discrimination. Proof is often difficult because there may be no direct evidence to be found. Tribunals are aware of this, however, and will generally be sympathetic towards a genuine applicant. If the tribunal decides unlawful discrimination has occurred, it can: award compensation, including a payment for injury to feelings; make an order declaring the rights of the parties; and make recommendations as to how the employer should alter his behaviour to bring an end to the discrimination within a specified time. Legal aid may be available for such tribunal cases (see chapter 21 on legal aid).

What about harassment at work?

This is when one person or a group's behaviour towards another gives offence, such as embarrassing remarks, cruel jokes or ridicule, unwelcome physical contact, sexual demands, racial shunning or ostracism or racial abuse. Employers can be liable for the actions of their workers at work or in a work-related situation (for example, at a social event) unless they can prove that they have taken all reasonable steps to prevent harassment occurring. You could make a claim of harassment to an Employment Tribunal under the Sex Discrimination Act 1975, Race Relations Act 1976 or Disability Discrimination Act 1995, and in respect of sexual orientation and/or religion.

Chapter 12

State Benefits

OR. A. LAFFERTY

How do I find my way through the benefits system?

You may be entitled to benefits if you are on a low income for a number of reasons, including your age, whether you are studying, or your family situation. Alternatively, you may receive some help if you have certain costs to meet, regardless of your income. The Department for Work and Pensions pays most benefits; however, your local authority manages council tax benefit and housing benefit, and the Inland Revenue administers tax credits. You have to meet certain conditions for any benefit that you wish to claim. Depending on your situation, you may be entitled to more than one type of benefit or tax credit. It is best to seek advice to make sure that you receive all the payments for which you qualify. If you do not get the benefits that you apply for, or your benefits are stopped, you may have the right to appeal to a Social Security Appeal Tribunal or a Medical Appeal Tribunal.

How can I get practical and/or legal advice on my claim?

The benefits system is often confusing and always changing. It is best to speak to a specialist adviser. Some solicitors (the Law Society of Scotland can advise you who is a good benefits solicitor) or your local Citizens' Advice Bureau will be able to provide you with up-to-date advice as to your entitlements and how to apply. Some areas have benefits advice offices or clinics or there are law centres in some towns and cities.

What if I am turned down for benefits?

You will receive a decision from the relevant office. If you are not satisfied, you should contact the office that made the decision. This should be done straight away by phone, letter or in person. You may ask for a verbal explanation and/or a written statement of reasons. If you are still not satisfied, you can ask them to look at the decision again. A new decision-maker will then look at your case. Alternatively, or following this step, you may be able to appeal to the Appeals Service. Strict time limits apply in every step of this procedure, so you cannot afford to waste any time. You must promptly fill in the form with full reasons for your appeal. You may wish to consult a legal expert at this stage. You must choose whether you would prefer to have an oral or a paper hearing. Following the hearing you will be given a decision notice, and you can request a statement of reasons. You are only able to appeal further, to the Social Security Commissioners, and from them to the Court of Session, on a point of law. If it is a fact that is under dispute, there are no further channels to pursue. Your decision letter from the Appeals Service will tell you how to appeal to the Commissioners.

How long does it take and how much does it cost to appeal?

The Social Security Appeal Tribunal is supposed to be significantly faster than the courts system. There are strict time limits that must be complied with by you and the Appeals Service in order to make the process as efficient as possible. Advice centres such as the Citizens' Advice Bureaux and law centres can assist you to fill in forms and letters free of charge. They may also provide you with representation at the tribunal. Trade unions may also offer free advice to members. The Appeals Service may pay some expenses (for example, travel fares) to enable you to attend the tribunal.

What if I have to go into a care home and I have savings or a house? Will benefits cover the cost of care?

Local authorities are largely responsible for funding the majority of older people in care. If you think that you may need help now or in the future paying for your care home, it is strongly advised that you ask for a needs assessment. This involves your local authority assessing your condition in order to provide a recommendation that you move into a care home. The local authority will then pay fees directly to the care home on your behalf. If you have savings greater than the upper limit (currently £18,500), you will be expected to refund the entire cost of the fees to the local authority. If your savings are less than this amount, but greater than the lower limit (currently £11,500) you will be expected to make a contribution based upon your income and savings. If your total savings are below the lower limit, they are ignored in all calculations. If you own your home, the value is usually counted as capital. There are exceptions to this, including if your husband or wife lives in the home, or if a close relative over the age of 60 or who is incapacitated lives there. However, even when your home is included as capital, you cannot be forced to sell the property. If you choose not to sell, and therefore cannot pay the assessed contribution, the money that you owe the local authority will mount up. This will continue until the house is eventually sold, or your estate is wound up. Then, the local authority will receive its payment. This is known as a 'deferred payments agreement'.

Chapter 13

Criminal Law and Procedure

What are the main crimes in Scotland?

There are so many crimes that they would fill a book by themselves; however, crimes fall into two main categories. The first category consists of common law crimes which are more traditional (for example, murder, culpable homicide, rape, robbery, fire-raising, theft, fraud and breach of the peace) and the second consists of statutory offences which have been created by Acts of Parliament (for example, possession of firearms, supply of controlled drugs, road traffic offences, income tax evasion and breach of the Official Secrets Act). Note that many actions can be criminal even if the crime intended is not successful, such as attempted theft, or, if a punch is swung but does not connect, the crime of attempted assault. There are also a great many United Kingdom and Scottish statutes that create a gigantic number and range of offences that are obscure or unusual to a greater or lesser degree, but punishable nonetheless. The following is a table of the main crimes and offences.

Crimes and offences

Abduction	Deprivation of a victim's personal liberty or unlawful detention.
Assault	Any attack upon the person of another. Attack has a very wide meaning and need not involve substantial violence, injury to the victim, or be direct (and see chapter 22 on self-defence).
Assault on a police officer and resisting arrest	Note that it still may be an offence to resist arrest by a police officer acting in the course of his duty, even if you are eventually acquitted of the charge he arrests you for.
Bestiality	Engaging in sexual activity with an animal.
Bigamy	Entering into a formally valid marriage with another while already married.
Breach of the peace	The ultimate all-embracing offence in Scots criminal law. At one time it did require some degree of disturbance of the public peace; it was then extended to encompass 'anything done in breach of public order or decorum which might reasonably be expected to lead to the lieges being alarmed or upset or tempted to make reprisals at their own hand'. A more modern definition is 'conduct which does present as genuinely alarming and disturbing, in its context, to any reasonable person'. The offence may be committed in private.
Careless driving	Driving on a public road without exercising due care and attention.
Carrying a knife	There are specific rules about sharp-bladed weapons found on or in the possession of a person in a public place.
Carrying an offensive weapon	Having a weapon in a public place is an offence unless there is a reasonable excuse for having it, such as for genuine work purposes.
Contempt of court	Can be described as conduct which challenges or affronts the authority of the court or the supremacy of the law itself, such as failure by a witness to appear before a court when required.

Culpable homicide:	A general but unsatisfactory comparison would be with English manslaughter. It covers situations where either there are mitigating circumstances, such as provocation or diminished responsibility, or where there is a degree of negligence or recklessness in conduct which is not sufficient to be murderous, but makes the homicide culpable nonetheless.
Dangerous driving (and causing death by dangerous driving)	Dangerous driving is essentially driving which falls below the standard to be expected of a competent and careful driver. If death is caused, then this is a separate and more serious offence under the Road Traffic Act.
Driving or using a vehicle without insurance	Note that it is your duty to check you are insured before driving, and it will not be a defence if you were casually advised by the car owner that the insurance covered you.
Driving under the influence of alcohol or drugs	This can be either driving while under the influence of drink or drugs, while unfit, or driving with excess amount of drink or drugs in your body.
Embezzlement	A form of theft, distinguished by the element of breach of trust in dealing with property, classically when an employee steals from his employer.
Escaping from lawful custody	Escaping detention or arrest by police or prison authorities.
Extortion	Commonly referred to as blackmail. Generally means making demands of another calculated to make that person act to their own or another's prejudice, supported by a threat which the person knows or believes may cause the other to accede to the demand.
Fire-raising	Essentially setting fire to the property of another person; now covers intentional fire-raising and reckless fire-raising
Forgery	Of itself it is not a crime; it is only when 'uttered' (tendered or used on a third party) that the crime is committed.
Fraud	Bringing about any practical result by means of false pretence.

Housebreaking	At common law, housebreaking is regarded as an aggravation to stealing or part of a preparatory offence, but is not an offence in itself (as in **Theft** or attempted theft by housebreaking).
Indecent assault	A wide-ranging term covering any personal physical attack or attempt characterised by some form of indecency.
Indecent exposure	Exposure of those parts of a person that are usually concealed, where exposure indicates an improper motive, or, where there is no sexual element, when it is done in a public place.
Malicious damage/ malicious mischief	Intentionally or recklessly destroying or damaging the property of another (also see **Vandalism**).
Misuse of drugs	Offences including possession, supply and smuggling of controlled drugs are charged under the Misuse of Drugs Act.
Murder	Causing the death of another person with the intention of causing that death, or with callous recklessness as to whether such a death is caused.
Perjury	Wilfully giving false evidence on oath or affirmation in any judicial proceedings.
Perverting the course of justice (or attempting to pervert the course of justice)	Covers a wide range of conduct, in criminal or civil proceedings, such as giving false statements to the police, intimidating witnesses or knowingly bringing false criminal charges against a person.
Rape (1)	When a man has sexual intercourse with a woman without her consent. The question of what constitutes consent, or the absence of it, is the subject of ongoing interpretation and argument in the courts.
Rape (2) ('constructive or statutory rape')	When a man has sexual intercourse with a girl under the age of 16, consent is immaterial. When the accused man is under the age of 24 and has had sexual intercourse with a girl aged between 13 and 16 , and if there are reasonable grounds for making an error as to her age, this may be a defence to the charge.

Reset (pronounced REE-set)	Receiving property dishonestly appropriated by another party. Knowledge, including a suspicion, that the origin of the property is by means of dishonest appropriation is an essential element. The common term is fencing.
Road traffic offences	There are some specific traffic offences in this list. Other common offences include: having bald tyres or defective equipment on a vehicle; failing to use tachograph records in a lorry; not wearing a seat-belt; not wearing a helmet on a motorbike; failing to stop after an accident; and driving while disqualified (also see chapter 14).
Robbery	**Theft** accomplished by means of personal violence or intimidation. It becomes a more serious offence when it is carried out armed.
Soliciting	Not being a solicitor, but loitering for the purposes of prostitution, or obtaining the services of a prostitute, in a public place or importuning (pestering) anyone in a public place.
Squatting	Camping on another person's land or squatting in someone's house without permission.
Taking and driving a vehicle without the owner's consent	Not only taking a car from the street, but driving a family member's car without their knowledge. This can be relevant for insurance purposes. If you did not have the consent of the owner, then you will not be covered by their insurance, or yours.
Tax offences	Carrying out activities or schemes which cause tax *evasion*. (Often mistaken for tax *avoidance*, which is legal. The difference is perhaps tricky to justify, but there is a long history of tax-saving schemes dreamed up by accountants for their clients being interpreted by the Inland Revenue as being clever but within the law, or else devious, and illegal! The former is called avoidance, the latter, evasion.)
Terrorism offences	A range of offences that include being involved in terrorism, assisting or supporting those who conduct terrorist activities.

Theft	Deliberately taking property belonging to someone else with a view to permanently depriving the rightful owner of it (note that temporary deprivation is still theft, but under proposals before the Scottish Parliament it may become a different but specific offence of criminal interference with property).
Threats (making unlawful threats)	Some threats are criminal in themselves; generally a threat is anything intending another person to believe that threat will be carried out.
Vandalism	Wilful or reckless damage or destruction of property without reasonable excuse.

What are the powers of the police to stop and question me?

The tradition of the law is that the police officers are ordinary citizens with no more rights than anyone else to order people about or detain them, except in particular circumstances. So if you are going about your lawful business and not committing crime, the police have no right to arrest you or make you tell them what you are doing. Police in reality, however, have serious duties to perform and need powers to allow them to do so, in order to protect the general freedom and peace to which everybody is entitled. Police powers fall into various categories, depending on the nature and extent of any emergency or threat to public order, safety or protection. If an officer is on duty and in uniform (or, if in plain clothes, identifies himself as a police officer by means of his warrant card), he can stop you and ask your name and address, and you are duty bound to give this information. He can only arrest you if he has a warrant to do so, or a reasonable suspicion that you have been involved in an arrestable criminal offence. If you are driving, the police can only stop you and question you if they reasonably consider that you have been drinking or that you have been involved in a moving traffic offence (or both), or are fleeing the scene of a crime you may be involved in. The police may question you, but for most purposes you retain a right to silence.

What if I reported a crime but now want to drop the charges?

Once a crime has been reported to the police or to the Procurator Fiscal it is no longer in your hands. The Procurator Fiscal prosecutes independently on behalf of the Crown, and in effect for the public good. They do not have to have the agreement of the victim of the crime to prosecute. You become simply a witness in the case, and indeed if you fail to come to court, refuse to give evidence or change your story, you may be charged with contempt of court or perjury (see the definitions above).

What if I witnessed a crime but no longer want to be involved in the case?

The only person with a right to silence is the accused. If you are cited as a witness (for either the prosecution or defence), then you must go to court, and once in the witness box you must answer all the questions, unless the answer to any question may incriminate you. There is an important exception to this in that a spouse cannot be compelled to give evidence against his or her spouse, unless the matter is an allegation of assault by that husband or wife on their spouse.

Am I entitled to one phone call at the police station if I am arrested?

No. You are entitled to have the officers call your solicitor or the duty solicitor to advise them of your arrest, but you may not make a call. You are entitled to have one other person or a solicitor informed of your arrest and a solicitor can attend and give you advice. If you do not have a solicitor then the duty solicitor can be contacted to come and advise you.

Am I entitled to have a solicitor with me at the police station?

If you are at the police station by way of voluntary attendance, or are arrested, you can have a solicitor called to the station to advise you and to be present during interviews. However, if you are detained under section 14 of the Criminal Procedure (Scotland) Act 1995, on reasonable suspicion of committing a crime punishable by imprisonment, but not yet charged with that offence, then the police can hold and question you for up to six hours. While you can have a member of family, a friend or a solicitor informed of your detention, you are not allowed to consult a lawyer. After that the police must release you, or arrest and charge you, in which case a solicitor can attend the station to give you advice, or release you.

Can the police fingerprint me, take personal details, and how long can they keep them?

The police can, if they reasonably consider it appropriate, take and use reasonable force to take, samples of hair, nails, finger or palm prints, fluid samples, or swabs from inside the mouth of persons arrested or detained and in police custody, or take information from that person. They must destroy them as soon as reasonably practical after a decision not to prosecute has been taken. If prosecution proceeds, the samples are not of course destroyed, though if you are acquitted they must then be destroyed.

What happens if I am charged with a crime?

If you are verbally charged by police, you have the right to make a reply, but this may be recorded or noted and used in evidence in court later at a trial. You have the right to remain silent, and should be cautioned (that is told of your rights). Thereafter, if the crime is serious, you may be held in the police station until the next court day, whether overnight or over a weekend. You will be served in the court cells with charge papers (either a complaint, or, if the case is more serious, a petition) and will then appear at court. There are different procedures depending on whether the case is by petition, which normally leads to a jury trial, or by a lower-level complaint, which leads to a trial in front of a magistrate or sheriff sitting without a jury.

Which court will my case be heard in?

The least serious cases are heard in the local district court presided over by a magistrate, more serious cases in the local sheriff court, and the most serious cases in the High Court of Justiciary, which may sit in your city, a nearby city, or in Edinburgh where it is based. Appeals from decisions of all criminal courts are heard in the Court of Criminal Appeal, which is within the High Court in Edinburgh.

Can I keep my case out of the papers?

No. The essence of our legal system is that courts are held in public, so justice can be done, and be seen to be done. Victims' identities are more often kept anonymous, especially child and rape victims, not accused persons. In some very unusual circumstances there may be an exception: for example where to identify the defendant will identify the victim, as in the case of incest.

Will I get legal aid to have a lawyer defend me at court?

If you appear direct from custody, having been arrested at a police station and brought to court, your initial representation is paid for under the duty solicitor scheme. If your case is a serious one on petition, the court has the power to grant legal aid there and then for the whole case. However, if the case is by summary complaint, through your solicitor you have to submit an application to the Scottish Legal Aid Board, which may or may not be granted. If it is granted it will cover your whole representation to the end of the case, which may be weeks or months later. If refused, then you will have to pay your solicitor private fees if you wish to be represented.

Can I defend myself?

You can represent yourself unless you are charged with a sexual offence, in which case you must be represented by a lawyer. If you do represent yourself and you are not a lawyer, you are automatically putting yourself at a disadvantage as you do not know the rules of criminal procedure or evidence. You could mistakenly allow in evidence that should be inadmissible, or you could fail to bring forward crucial evidence of your own. If a legal point were to come up, you may not know how to argue it. Sheriffs, magistrates and judges will provide assistance, at least to the point of ensuring fairness to an accused person, and should show patience when he or she makes procedural errors or is unsure of what to do, but they are not obliged to help a party to run their case in court.

Can I insist on trial by jury?

No, the decision as to the court and procedure belongs solely to the Crown in Scotland. In general, the more serious the crime charged, the more likely it is to be in front of a jury, and some crimes, such as robbery, rape and murder, are inevitably on solemn procedure, as jury trials are called. Even in this area there are divisions. The worst crimes, such as murder and rape, are tried in the High Court, whereas other crimes and offences (drug crimes, for example) can be heard by a jury either in the sheriff court or the High Court. The choice of forum is for the Crown, and will depend on factors such as the seriousness of the particular crime (if drugs, the amount of heroin or cocaine involved will be relevant) and the record of the accused. The worse the crime, and the more regular the offender, the more likely it will be to go to a higher court.

Who can be on a jury, and who is disqualified? How can I get out of being on a jury?

Men and women between the ages of 18 and 65 on the electoral roll are eligible for jury service. If cited to attend, you must do so, otherwise you commit an offence and can be punished, even if you do not want to be on a jury for whatever reason. Some professionals who are exempt are judges, lawyers, some social workers, police and Children's Panel officials. Also exempt are those suffering from a mental disorder and most people who have been in prison. Some people in essential services can elect to be exempt when cited, such as doctors, vets, nurses and members of the armed forces. If you are not exempt, but have a serious excuse, such as illness, pre-arranged holidays, or special work commitments, you may contact the clerk of court to seek to be excused.

How is a jury selected in court?

Once the members of the assize (that is all those cited to attend for jury service) are assembled in the court and a case is called, the clerk of the court has all the names on folded pieces of paper in a glass bowl, and pulls them out, like a raffle. The names are read out and the persons named come forward and take their seat in the jury box. The lawyers for prosecution and defence can object to the election of members if they can show a good reason why a person should not serve on a case. Note there are 15 people on a Scottish jury, and not 12 people as in England.

Can I object to certain people being selected to sit on a jury in my case?

Your lawyer has rights to object to persons balloted from the assize to sit on a jury. For either prosecution or defence to object successfully, however, good cause must be shown. Good cause would include where the juror knows the accused, is related to an alleged victim, or lives two doors from the scene of the alleged offence. You cannot object because the person is a teacher, elderly or a woman, for example.

How does a jury decide a case?

After hearing the evidence from witnesses and the summing-up speeches from prosecution and defence lawyers, and a legal charge or set of instructions from the sheriff or judge, the jury retires into secret session and considers how to decide the case. No one is allowed to interfere or advise, and no one is allowed to question the actings or decisions of the jury before, during, or after its deliberations. It can give one of three verdicts for each accused and each charge before it: guilty, not guilty or not proven. Both not guilty and not proven are acquittals, and are final. There is no substantial difference between the two forms of acquittal, though the not proven verdict remains controversial. A bare majority is enough to convict, unlike in England where the jury must all agree.

Do I have to give evidence if I am on trial?

If you are accused, you are not obliged to 'take the stand'. It is up to the Crown to prove its case. You are innocent until proved guilty beyond reasonable doubt. If the Crown has not enough credible and reliable evidence of the crime, then you have nothing to prove and must be acquitted. However, things are often not so black and white in court, and it is a matter of expert professional judgment by your lawyer or legal team as to whether it is better to give evidence or not. The decision is yours, but you should listen to the advice given.

What is the range of punishments open to our courts?

The main division of punishments is between custodial and non-custodial disposals. Custody is of course prison, or a young offenders institution for persons under 21. Sentences can vary from a few days to the rest of your life, depending on the seriousness of the case and the extent of your own criminal record, if any. The court may get social enquiry reports, psychiatric reports and/or other material to help it decide the appropriate disposal. The following table shows the most common non-custodial disposals.

Non-custodial disposals

Absolute discharge	The most lenient disposal which is only granted exceptionally. It is simply a marking of the finding of guilt, and does not count as a conviction against your record.

Admonition	A marking of the finding of guilt that *does* count to your record.
Community service	An order forcing you to do unpaid work to benefit the community. It may be gardening at a local park, domestic duties in a care home, or clearing up rubbish on a river. It must be done within 12 months, and failure to carry out the tasks, or not showing up when required, can mean being brought back to court in front of the same judge and being given an alternative punishment.
Confiscation of goods or assets	Where those goods or assets have been used for the commission of a crime or are the proceeds of crime (especially in drugs cases).
Deferred sentence	Where sentence is deferred by the court to allow you to show that you can behave properly, and, if so, this will cause the court to deal more leniently with you when you return to court with a good report.
Disqualification	From driving and penalty points on a driving licence.
Electronic tagging	What is in effect a mobile radio is attached, to the ankle usually, which signals to a control office where you are. If you are in the wrong place (for example, out of your house at night when you should be at home) you can be found out, and, if so breaching the order, can be brought back to court to be dealt with by a different disposal.
Fines	Can either be at the discretion of the judge or subject to scales laid down by statute; criminal compensation payable through the court to the victim of your crime.
Probation	You must not offend during the period, which may be months or even years, and must report to a probation officer as often as required. If you offend or fail to report, the case can be sent back to the court for an alternative disposal to be given out. The probation order can have additional conditions imposed, such as attendance for drug therapy or drink counselling.

Restriction of rights	Someone convicted of animal abuse may be disqualified from owning a dog, or a fraudster may be no longer entitled to be a company director.
Sex Offenders Register	Placement on the register for a period of time set by the court on conviction of a sex offence. You must register at the local police office and any change of address must be notified.
Special projects	There is a range of special projects usually linked to probation which may be to assist you in dealing with alcohol or other addictions.

If I am dissatisfied with the verdict in my case or the punishment I receive, can I appeal?

Both conviction and sentence can be appealed. Appeals from decisions of all criminal courts are heard in the High Court in Edinburgh. If you are appealing against a conviction, the appeal court will not re-hear the evidence (though it may hear fresh evidence in exceptional circumstances), assuming a jury or a sheriff hearing the witnesses at first hand has acted reasonably in deciding to accept certain evidence and reject other evidence. If there has been unfairness, oppression, or a miscarriage of justice in the original case, then the High Court may overturn the conviction. In some cases a retrial may even be ordered. Appeals against sentence can be heard on their own or in tandem with an appeal against conviction. The court may not necessarily reduce or change a sentence in favour of the accused, but can in some cases increase it, so it is a matter of judgment, not to say risk, as to whether to appeal as it may go against you. Appeals are not automatically heard by the full court in Edinburgh; they go through a sifting process by a single judge to weed out cases without any merit at all. If you have been convicted and sentenced to prison, you can ask to be freed pending your appeal, but this is not an automatic right. This is called interim liberation.

What if I am then dissatisfied with the appeal?

You can ask for your case to be reviewed by the Scottish Criminal Cases Review Commission. The process is best started by asking your solicitor to advise you and make the application.

Do previous convictions always have to be disclosed, or do they expire?

Some convictions, although they remain on your criminal record, do not have to be mentioned by you in some situations; this is called rehabilitation of offenders. See the table below for some of the main qualifications. If your conviction is spent, that is, was before the rehabilitation cut-off point dictated by the law, then it does not have to be mentioned if you apply for some jobs, a mortgage, insurance or finance. However, the rights do not apply if you are applying for certain jobs: for example, as an accountant, lawyer, doctor, nurse, dentist, prison officer, traffic warden, social worker, teacher or any job that involves looking after children. You must also disclose convictions if you are applying for a firearms or gaming licence. Spent convictions can also be revealed in any conviction in a subsequent court case against you. It is an offence for a person in an official capacity to reveal your spent conviction, and, if a newspaper maliciously reveals your spent conviction, it could be sued for defamation.

Spent convictions

Punishment	Rehabilitation
Imprisonment for 6 months to 2.5 years	10 years
Prison for up to 6 months	7 years
Fine, community service order	5 years
Probation	1 year
Absolute discharge	6 months

(Note: some of these periods are cut in half if the offender was 17 years of age when the offence occurred.)

Chapter 14

Road Traffic Cases

A. LAFFERTY

Can I appeal against a fixed penalty notice?

You can write to the initiating authority and say you do not accept the penalty, or simply do nothing and await the service of a complaint (known informally as a summons) from the Procurator Fiscal. You then have the right to plead not guilty to the charge against you, defend yourself or be defended, and contest the prosecution evidence at a trial.

Can police stop me while driving?

You can be stopped or waved down by police acting in the course of their duties if you are reasonably suspected of having committed a moving traffic offence; are fleeing the scene of a crime that you may have been involved in; or if you are suspected of having alcohol in your body. It does not need to be excess alcohol for police to be able to stop you.

What offences will get me disqualified from driving?

A more or less automatic ban arises if you are convicted of driving with excess alcohol or driving unfit through drink or drugs; if you refuse without reasonable excuse to give a police officer a sample of breath, blood or urine; if you drive while already disqualified from driving for some other offence; for dangerous (reckless) driving; or for causing death by dangerous driving. The court can also use its discretion to disqualify you for some other road traffic offences if they are serious enough, or you are a persistent offender. Note that along with disqualification you can be fined, or, in the more serious cases, such as causing death by dangerous driving, you can be imprisoned.

If I am banned from driving, can I get my licence back?

If you are banned from driving for less than two years, you cannot apply for the disqualification to be lifted. If you are banned for less than four years, you can apply after you have served two years of the ban. If the ban is for between four and ten years, you can apply once you have served half of it. If the ban is longer than that, you can apply after five years. The application is by a written petition to the sheriff court or High Court: the court considers factors such as any criminal convictions since the imposition of the ban; the nature of the offence(s) causing it; and any other circumstances – for example, that you have stopped drinking alcohol or that you have a job opportunity involving driving that will alleviate financial hardship. The court is not bound to give you your licence back, and may refuse a petition.

Which offences merit endorsements/penalty points?

There is a whole range of offences. Some offences allow the court to use its discretion to award a higher or lower number of points depending on how serious the offence is, whereas some have mandatory numbers. Below is a table of the main offences, their DVLA codes and the endorsements that are applicable. Remember that, although some offences show a number of penalty points that would not of itself mean automatic disqualification, the court may, and often does, disqualify drivers for serious road traffic offending such as drink driving, driving whilst disqualified and dangerous driving.

Code	Accident offences	Penalty points
AC10	Failing to stop after an accident	5–10
AC20	Failing to give particulars or to report an accident within 24 hours	5–10

Code	Disqualified driver	Penalty points
BA10	Driving while disqualified by order of Court	6
	Careless driving	
CD10	Driving without due care and attention	3–9
CD20	Driving without reasonable consideration for other road users	3–9
CD30	Driving without due care and attention or without reasonable consideration for other road users	3–9
	Construction and use offences	
CU10	Using a vehicle with defective brakes	3
CU20	Causing, or likely to cause, danger by reason of use of unsuitable vehicle or using a vehicle with parts or accessories (excluding brakes, steering or tyres) in a dangerous condition	3
CU30	Using a vehicle with defective tyres	3
CU40	Using a vehicle with defective steering	3
CU50	Causing or likely to cause danger by reason of load or passengers	3
CU60	Undefined failure to comply with Road Vehicles (Construction and Use) Regulations	3
	Dangerous driving	
DD40	Dangerous driving	3–11
DD60	Culpable homicide while driving a car	3–11
DD70	Causing death by reckless driving	3–11
	Drink or drugs	
DR10	Driving or attempting to drive with alcohol level above limit	3–11
DR20	Driving or attempting to drive while unfit through drink or drugs	3–11

Code	Drink or drugs	Penalty points
DR30	Driving or attempting to drive then refusing to supply a specimen for analysis	3–11
DR40	In charge of a vehicle while alcohol level above limit	10
DR50	In charge of a vehicle while unfit through drink	10
DR80	Driving or attempting to drive when unfit through drugs	3–11
DR90	In charge of a vehicle when unfit through drugs	10
DR60	In charge of a vehicle then refusing to supply a specimen for analysis	10
DR70	Failing to provide specimen for breath test	4
	Insurance offences	
IN10	Using a vehicle uninsured against third party risks	6–8
	Licence offences	
LC10	Driving without a licence	4–8
	Miscellaneous offences	
MS10	Leaving a vehicle in a dangerous position	3
MS20	Unlawful pillion riding	1
MS40	Driving with uncorrected defective eyesight or refusing to submit to a test	3
MS50	Motor racing on the highway	3–11
	Motorway offences	
MW10	Contravention of Special Roads Regulations (excluding speed limits)	3
	Pedestrian crossings	
PC10	Undefined contravention of Pedestrian Crossing Regulations	3

Code	Pedestrian crossings	Penalty points
PC20	Contravention of Pedestrian Crossing Regulations with a moving vehicle	3
PC30	Contravention of Pedestrian Crossing Regulations with a stationary vehicle	3
	Provisional licence offences	
PL10	Driving without 'L' plates	2
PL20	Not accompanied by a qualified person	2
PL30	Carrying a person not qualified	2
PL40	Drawing an unauthorised trailer	2
PL50	Undefined failure to comply with conditions of a provisional licence	2
	Speed limits	
SP10	Exceeding goods vehicle speed limits	3–6
SP20	Exceeding speed limit for type of vehicle (excluding goods or passenger vehicles)	3–6
SP30	Exceeding statutory speed limit	3–6
SP40	Exceeding passenger vehicle speed limit	3–6
SP50	Exceeding speed limit on motorway	3–6
SP60	Undefined speed limit offence	3–6
	Traffic directions signs	
TS10	Failing to comply with traffic light signals	3
TS20	Failing to comply with double white lines	3
TS30	Failing to comply with a 'stop' sign	3
TS40	Failing to comply with direction of a constable or traffic warden	3
TS50	Failing to comply with a traffic sign (excluding stop signs, traffic lights or double white lines)	3

Code	Traffic directions signs	Penalty points
TS60	Failing to comply with a school crossing patrol sign	3
TS70	Undefined failure to comply with a traffic direction or sign	3
	Theft or unauthorised taking	
UT10	Taking and driving away a vehicle without consent or an attempt thereat	8
UT20	Stealing or attempting to steal a vehicle	8
UT30	Going equipped for stealing or taking a vehicle	8
UT40	Taking or attempting to take a vehicle without consent; driving or attempting to drive a vehicle knowing it to have been taken without consent; allowing oneself to be carried in or on a vehicle knowing it to have been taken without consent	8

How does totting-up disqualification happen?

Once you have reached 12 points for various offences on your licence within a period of three years, you will automatically be disqualified for a minimum of six months. There is an exception open to the court if disqualification would cause severe hardship, and there are mitigating circumstances. However, losing a job, or working far from home in unsociable hours will usually *not* be enough to allow you to escape a ban. New drivers should note that if you are within two years of passing your test and reach six points, you are disqualified until you re-sit your test.

When can I refuse to give a breath, blood or urine test?

You can only refuse either a police roadside breath test, an electronic test at a police station, or a blood or urine test if you were clearly not driving nor in charge of a vehicle, and there was no reasonable suspicion that you were. However, if there is such suspicion and it turns out to be incorrect, you may still be guilty of the offence of failing to give a specimen unless you have a reasonable excuse such as physically or mentally being unable to give a specimen. You would need to lead medical evidence at court of any such condition.

If I am caught on speed camera, do I have to admit I was the driver?

Yes. Where the driver of a vehicle is alleged to be guilty of a traffic offence, the vehicle's registered keeper must give such information as to the identity of the driver as he may be required by the police. This requirement was recently challenged in the courts on the basis that it infringed the right to a fair trial as it denied the suspect the right to silence and the right against self-incrimination. The courts decided that the right against self-incrimination is not absolute; it has to be balanced against the clear public interest in the enforcement of road traffic legislation for road safety. Therefore, there is no defence for a refusal to admit to being the driver of a vehicle when a motoring offence is committed.

Can I use my mobile phone while driving?

From December 2003 it has been an offence to use your phone, unless with a safe hands-free kit, while driving a vehicle. The fine is £30 or, if prosecuted, up to £1,000 and three penalty points.

If I am involved in an accident must I report it to the police, or is it enough to swap insurance details with the other driver?

The law, strictly speaking, is that any accident in which you are a participant should be reported to the police as soon as possible, and at least within 24 hours of the accident. If it is a minor bump, with no personal injuries, the police may not be interested in getting a report. However, my clear advice is to report all accidents and not to take that chance. This is for two reasons: one is that you run the risk of committing the offence of failing to report an accident; and secondly, you cannot guarantee the other driver will not report the accident to the police, making you look as if you have something to hide. In addition, your insurance company may very well insist that you report the accident, and you may be in breach of your policy if you do not.

Chapter 15

Civil Law and Procedure

What does civil law include?

Civil law includes various branches of Scots law: for example, buying and selling houses, family law, accident claims, breach of contract, debt and executries. It involves the rights and duties in legal relationships between any combination of private citizens, corporate and public bodies, and how these can be resolved when things go wrong, or just to make sure they keep on the straight and narrow.

How do I enforce my rights in civil law?

You can go to court or to a tribunal. In some situations, it may be advantageous to try to reach an agreement with the other party as an alternative or before taking legal action. Some contracts may provide that mediation or arbitration must be undertaken before any court proceedings can be raised. Your solicitor will advise you as to the best course of action.

How does legal aid work in civil disputes?

Legal aid provides assistance for individuals who may otherwise be unable to afford access to the legal system. Sometimes advice and representation are provided at no cost, but depending upon your financial position you may have to provide a contribution. If you think you may be entitled to financial assistance, look out for the legal aid symbol when finding a solicitor. Not all solicitors are registered to take on legal aid cases. There are two kinds of legal aid: Advice and Assistance covers advice on any matter of Scots law, and general work done by a solicitor, such as consultations, correspondence, drawing up documents. However, this does not normally cover most representation in court. Should your case proceed to court, you may require civil legal aid. This is funding that will enable your solicitor to take your case to court and see it through to the end. It can cover expenses such as case preparation, the hearing and any fees for advocates and expert witnesses. Legal aid is not automatically provided. You will be required to give your solicitor accurate current information on your financial position, including income and savings and any dependants, so that the Scottish Legal Aid Board can assess: (a) your financial position; and (b) the legal basis of your case, and decide whether it is reasonable in the circumstances to award legal aid.

How are civil court orders enforced?

The enforcement of civil court orders is a private matter, meaning that responsibility falls upon the parties involved rather than the state. The court order is a decree containing a warrant for execution; this is the authority to enforce what is stated in the order. An official copy of this authority must be extracted from the court books. The individual or the solicitor relying upon the order sends the extract to the Messengers-at-Arms or sheriff officers to act in the enforcement. You will have to pay the sheriff officers' fees and seek to recover them from the opponent as part of the process. The ways in which civil obligations are enforced vary depending on the type of order. Some orders involve the payment of money, while others may be for the residence (custody) of children. The court officer may enforce the order by a variety of means including: attachment and diligence against earnings; forcibly entering premises if necessary; or enforcing the delivery of a child under court order.

What kinds of civil court action are there?

The divisions of civil cases are generally along financial limits. For cases in which a sum up to £750 is in dispute, the *small claims* court in the sheriff court is the only forum available. For cases between £750 and £1,500, the *summary cause* court (again in the sheriff court) is where cases are heard. For actions greater than £1,500 and for non-financial actions, such as divorce, paternity or a declarator of occupancy rights, the *ordinary* sheriff court procedure applies. There are also other kinds of specialised action in the sheriff court, including summary applications for people appealing against orders such as the cancellation of a licence, or a case under the

Representation of the People Act (where someone wants to complain about the conduct of an election). The sheriff courts are local, that is they are tied to the county in which they are located. The Court of Session is a unitary court that is situated in Edinburgh, and is generally used where there are very large sums of money involved. No matter which court in which you sue, or are sued, the case is based on written pleadings drawn up stating the case and the defence. There may be legal arguments heard at a debate, and eventually a hearing of facts and evidence, known as a proof. There can be various other procedures ordered by the court to investigate points of law or fact to help in the case. Eventually the presiding sheriff or judge issues a judgment in the form of an interlocutor, either granting decree in favour of the pursuer or the defender. A case can be partially or fully won. If the defender wins, he gets either a dismissal or *absolvitor*. The loser usually has to pay his own court costs and those of the winning opponent. No matter which court you end up in, it is usually a slow and painful business.

How do I take a small claim to court?

The small claims court is at the sheriff court. There are rules about jurisdiction that decide which town's court should be used, but often it will be your local court that hears the case. It is a court in which minor legal claims (with values up to £750) and disputes are supposed to be dealt with more quickly, efficiently and cheaply than larger cases, which can take months or years to get through and involve very high costs. The idea is that a pursuer who is making a claim or seeking an order from the court can complete a straightforward form, with the help of the sheriff clerk at the court office, and appear at a hearing to argue the case if the defender contests it. If it is contested by the defender, the court usually has two hearings. The first is a preliminary hearing to establish what is in dispute and what is not, in the hope of getting the case settled or resolved there and then; or, if not, a second hearing is fixed, which may be a hearing of evidence and/or legal argument. There are court leaflets to assist persons pursuing or defending small claims cases.

Do I need or get a lawyer for a small claim case?

Anyone going to court without a lawyer takes a risk. Although the sums disputed in small claims cases are by definition minor, the legal points and arguments that apply can be just as important as those involving larger sums. However, in an effort to put people off employing lawyers, who may complicate cases and put off unrepresented opponents, the costs that can be awarded to a successful party are very limited. If the value of the claim is not more than £200, then no legal expenses can be awarded. For other small claim cases, the maximum expenses that can be awarded are £75. The sheriff can be asked to award expenses on a variety of grounds, and can punish a party who has behaved unreasonably in the way he has conducted the case.

Do I need to bring witnesses to a small claims hearing?

Witnesses do not need to attend the preliminary hearing, but if the sheriff fixes a proof (a hearing in which evidence is to be taken) then it is up to you to ensure the right witnesses come to court. If they are cited properly to do so, then the citation has the effect of a court order forcing them to come, and they can be punished and held in contempt of court if they fail to appear. You are liable for your own witnesses' costs unless the court orders your opponent to pay these. If you do not cite them, or get sheriff officers to do so, the court may hear the case without them and you will lose the benefit of their evidence. If both pursuer and defender agree the terms of some evidence, then a joint statement can be given to the court instead of bringing the witness(es) along in person, thus saving both time and money.

What if I get a small claim court order and the other side won't pay up?

A decree from the small claims court has the same legal effect as any other court decree, and can be enforced by way of sheriff officers carrying out arrestment and/or attachment. As with ordinary cases, you will need to pay the sheriff officers and seek to recover their costs in the enforcement process.

Can I get legal aid to fight a small claim action?

Civil legal aid is not available to any small claims litigant to pay for a lawyer to represent him in court. However, Advice and Assistance is available for a pursuer or defender, subject to the usual financial qualifications, to allow him to instruct a solicitor or get advice in the case or to assist in preparation. Note that the legal aid rules make it necessary for any money recovered as a result of the solicitor's help to be put towards the legal aid fees incurred, unless the Scottish Legal Aid Board grants a hardship waiver.

What are the differences between a small claim and a summary cause?

Summary cause actions are for civil disputes in which the sum disputed is between £750 and £1,500. They are not unlike small claims in that there is a system of rules and procedures to make them as efficient and cost-efficient as possible, and less expensive, slow and complex than ordinary actions. Some preliminary and administrative hearings are presided over by the sheriff clerk rather than the sheriff, but, as with other procedures, if there is a dispute about facts, a proof will be fixed and evidence heard and the sheriff will make a decision in favour of one party or the other. Unlike small claims, it is likely that expenses will be awarded against all unsuccessful parties, and there is a special set of fees fixed for summary causes. Legal aid can be available for summary causes on the usual basis.

Who pays the costs of court actions generally if a party is not legally-aided?

Usually the winner gets his judicial expenses awarded to him, to be paid by the loser. This does not include legal fees incurred before the court action started, nor any part of the expenses found against him during the action. It is a matter for the judge to decide if all or only some of the costs should be awarded. Perhaps the winner caused unnecessary court work by failing to lodge appropriate papers or refusing to give information which would have saved time and effort. There is a special situation in which if the defender is sued for money, and offers a settlement by tender (a sealed written offer not seen by the judge), then the pursuer will bear the costs if his compensation award does not beat that figure (see chapter 10 on 'beating the tender').

What if I don't agree with a judgment of the court?

You can of course appeal. From any sheriff court *interlocutor*, you can appeal to the Sheriff Principal of the sheriffdom in which the court sits, or to the Inner House of the Court of Session in Edinburgh. Appeals from the decision of a single judge of the Court of Session (Outer House) are to the Court of Session's Inner House, where three judges hear the appeal. Appeals are usually on points of law, the disgruntled party seeking to persuade the appeal court that the judge of first instance decided the point or points incorrectly and as such should be overturned. There is a further appeal to the House of Lords in London. Although it is situated in England, it is made up of a mixture of English and Scottish judges. It is our highest domestic civil court. The Law Lords sit as an appeal court (unusually without wigs and gowns). Very occasionally there may be a further appeal to the European Court. Legal aid may be available to appeal on the usual basis. At the time of writing there is a proposal in Parliament at Westminster to institute a Supreme Court to replace the House of Lords' judicial role.

What is judicial review?

This is a specialised kind of civil case in which you sue the government or a public body for acting in a way that defeats your legal rights. There are innumerable examples of such actions: one example is as follows. When the criminal injuries compensation scheme was originally set up awards to victims were calculated on a case-by-case basis according to the traditional principles of (English) civil damages law. The government wanted to streamline the system (that is, save money) and unilaterally brought in a tariff system of awards, in which every injury had a set sum accruing from it. The Fire Brigades Union challenged this, and went to court for judicial review against the government on the basis that the right to criminal injuries compensation could not be changed without a new Act of Parliament. The government lost the case and the old system was put back in place. Although the government lost the battle, they won the war. The government then changed the law with an Act of Parliament, and we now have a tariff system of compensation for victims of violence once again. Legal aid is available for judicial review.

Chapter 16

Mental Ill-health and Physical Incapacity

What happens when someone becomes insane or unable mentally to act responsibly for themselves?

There are procedures under the Mental Health Act 1983 for a person suffering from metal illness, who is in danger or unfit to look after themselves, to be certified. Two doctors have to give reports confirming unfitness and the court will 'section' the patient, to be detained in an appropriate medical care facility. This procedure is only carried out in emergency or extreme situations. It can be contested by the patient, who can have a lawyer acting for them. Once the sectioning is no longer necessary it can be removed.

If someone is physically incapacitated but mentally fit, how can he carry out financial or other business?

He can grant a power of attorney to a trusted individual; they can be a friend, family member, solicitor or other professional. The power of attorney is a deed that gives legal authority to that person to act on behalf of the incapacitated one, and specifies the individual areas of responsibility, such as signing documents, dealing with bank accounts, paying bills and selling property. It is best to make the deed very specific and not open-ended. The power of attorney can be cancelled at any time by the person granting it; however, acts carried out while it is in force will remain binding. The attorney can be held to account for his stewardship. If the arrangement is what the law now calls a 'continuing power of attorney', it can be registered with the Office of the Public Guardian to supervise. Alternatively a guardian can be appointed by court order to carry out functions on behalf of the *incapax*, as he is properly called (see also the following answer).

Who represents or acts for someone who is mentally unfit?

Under the Adults with Incapacity (Scotland) Act 2000 a guardian can be appointed to look after the physical welfare and/or the financial affairs of an adult needing assistance. The person to be appointed must apply to the court or have an application made for him, and, if the sheriff at the hearing thinks it is appropriate, the guardian will be given authority to take over the care and management of the adult's affairs. The appointment can be permanent or for a set time and can be limited in the powers it contains. The guardianship can be recalled or terminated if it is no longer appropriate; this could be due to a number of reasons, including mismanagement by the guardian or the recovery of the adult.

How can a person acting as a guardian or attorney be accountable for their actions?

The guardian or person with continuing power of attorney has to report to the Office of the Public Guardian, and in financial cases must lodge financial reports and accounts with the Accountant of Court to make sure he is looking after the interests of the adult appropriately. Where welfare issues are concerned, the local mental health officer may also be involved in monitoring. If a third party such as a family member or friend is unhappy with the way a guardian or attorney is acting, he may report him to the Public Guardian, the local social work department or mental health officer.

Chapter 17

Debts

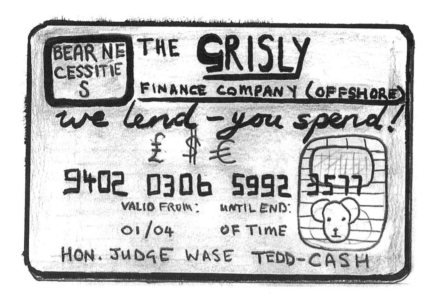

Can I be imprisoned for debt?

No, *except* when there has been wilful non-payment of maintenance after separation or divorce but mainly the only sanctions for debt are financial ones. These include arrestment of wages; arrestment of bank accounts (if there is anything in them when arrestment takes place); processes called attachment to take your goods and sell them; and also bankruptcy/sequestration. You could only face imprisonment if you wilfully obstruct any of these procedures or fail to co-operate with a bankruptcy trustee who is acting under the authority of the court.

If I have a joint debt, overdraft or account with someone else, do we each only have to pay a half?

The creditor can insist on payment from either or both of you. Most joint debts to banks and companies are *joint and several*, which allows the creditor to sue debtor A for the whole thing, leaving that debtor to recover half from debtor B. Debtor A cannot insist on paying only half the debt to the creditor.

Am I liable for my wife, husband or child's debt?

Not if it was taken out in their name alone. If you sign a guarantee for a debt, however, then you may be made to pay (in full) if the debtor defaults. You then have a right to sue the debtor for repayment to you.

If I sign a guarantee for someone else's debt, what are the circumstances in which I will have to pay?

If the debtor defaults you may have to pay. Most guarantees give the creditor the option to sue the guarantor without having to sue the debtor first, or he can sue both together. As a guarantor, you have a right to seek repayment from the main creditor.

If I am in financial difficulties, can I get debts/interest frozen?

Only if the creditor agrees, otherwise your contract of loan or other credit will almost certainly allow the creditor to keep adding interest against the loan until it is repaid, whether or not you are continuing to make payments.

How can I protect myself from creditors if my debts are overwhelming?

If you cannot find a solution to repaying your debts then you can seek sequestration, otherwise known as bankruptcy. See the next question for the processes.

How can I be made or become bankrupt?

If your debts are more than £1,500, and you have a decree and civil charge against you, you can get a solicitor to apply to the court for your own sequestration. If you don't have a decree, but can get creditors to agree, you can ask an insolvency specialist (who may be an accountant or a solicitor) to create a formal trust deed for creditors, which mirrors some of the effects and protections of a sequestration. In both of these procedures, the trustee becomes the legal owner of your property, and as long as you obey the instructions of the trustee and pay whatever limited amounts are due to him or her, you will be discharged after three years with your debts extinguished. You may be required to sell any assets that you have. If you own a house jointly with a spouse, he or she may be required to buy you out of your share to prevent the house being sold by order of the court on the application of the trustee.

How can I find out if I am on a credit blacklist?

Make contact with the company that has refused you credit as they are bound to give you the name and address of the credit reference company they used to check your credit. You can write to the credit reference company and pay a fee of around £2 to that agency to get a copy of their entry on you.

If the information is wrong, how can I get it corrected?

You can insist that the agency corrects a wrong entry, and if they fail to do so, you can write to the Director General of Fair Trading to complain. See the useful contacts section.

Can credit companies see my bank details?

Your credit file contains a variety of information that allows a credit company to confirm your identification and address. The file also enables the company to assess how you have managed any previous or existing credit agreements before they make the decision of whether to accept your application. Remember that no credit company is under any legal obligation to do business with you if they choose not to. The file includes:

- Electoral Roll information;
- decrees and bankruptcy information;
- bankruptcy details (these will be kept on file for six years);
- payment history information (this will include all financial agreements from the last two years); and
- information from banks, mobile phone companies, insurance companies and retailers may be detailed.

Basically, all recent incidents where you have been given credit are included.

What happens if I am taken to court for debt?

Your creditor must issue you with a default notice before taking you to court. You will then receive a sheriff court citation. It will contain a 'time to pay direction' to allow you a chance to pay the sum due without court action continuing. If you choose to do so, you should include details of your offer of payment within 21 days to the sheriff court (there are instructions on the forms provided to you). If your offer is accepted, a decree with time to pay will be granted. There can be no further court action unless your payments are not maintained. If you intend to contest the court proceedings, complete the 'deny the claim – intention to appear' form. You must include your reasons for disputing the claim. Sometime later on you will have to appear at court in person, and are advised to seek representation. If the matter goes to proof, you and others may be required to give evidence. If you do not respond at all to this initial writ, a decree (this is the Scottish term; it is referred to as a Civil Court Judgment or CCJ in England) will be granted against you; formal debt enforcement can follow.

Can a creditor remove my property for debt?

No. Before any court action commences, a creditor initially only has the right to remind you that you owe him money. If this does not prompt you to make payment, he must go to court to seek repayment. A creditor has no right personally to remove your property at any stage in the proceedings, nor does any agent or debt collector.

Do I have to deal with debt collectors and let them into my house?

Creditors sometimes appoint debt collectors (who go under a number of different guises, sometimes dressing up their letters as if they are official ones from solicitors) to collect money that is owed to them. Debt collectors must behave properly and are subject to standards laid down by the Office of Fair Trading. Similar to creditors, they are entitled to discreetly remind you that you owe money to the creditors. They are not allowed to cause you alarm, distress or humiliation. They are prohibited from attempting contact with you at unreasonable times and at unreasonable intervals. They may telephone your house or visit in person. However, you are not obliged to let them enter your home, nor need you give them financial information of any sort.

What powers do sheriff officers have?

Sheriff officers have the legal responsibility of enforcing sheriff court decrees. Enforcement in Scotland is called diligence. If payment is not made following a court action, the sheriff officers are instructed by the creditor. Initially, they will serve a 'charge for payment' upon you. They will visit you and demand payment of the sum due, with interest and expenses, within 14 days. If you do not pay, the sheriff officers can rely upon the common forms of diligence. These are arrestment of earnings, arrestment of bank accounts and/or attachment. The sheriff court will only grant what is called an Exceptional Attachment Order if certain conditions are satisfied. If granted, the sheriff officers can go to your house and remove non-essential assets. These will then be auctioned and sold. Essential assets include various items such as clothing, toys, beds and food.

Can my goods be taken away by sheriff officers if I am sued?

This would be a last resort. An attachment can poind (pronounced *pinned*) certain goods owned solely by the debtor, including a car valued in excess of £1,000 (remember this does not include cars on hire purchase or lease as they are owned by the finance company); tools of trade over £1,000; a mobile home (other than a principal residence); and commercial goods.

There are very strict rules controlling the activities of creditors and sheriff officers in carrying out diligence, and if they overstep the mark, the debtor can go to court to ask for an attachment to be cancelled for wrongful diligence.

What is a warrant sale?

Warrant sales have been abolished. The Attachment Order and the Exceptional Attachment Order have replaced the warrant sale. The Exceptional Attachment Order applies to consumers and provides a greater level of protection than the alternative. This is because it involves arrestment of items in peoples' homes, rather than assets in a business. Before granting this order the sheriff must be satisfied that all possible alternatives have been exhausted.

If I run up mortgage arrears, will my house automatically be repossessed?

It used to be that the law did not allow for any flexibility in this. If your arrears were over a certain amount this triggered the building society or bank's right to issue a default notice and then carry out the calling-up procedure leading to a decree against you. Eviction took place after that. Nothing except full payment of arrears, outstanding interest and legal costs would stop it. Under the Mortgage Rights (Scotland) Act 2001, however, you as a borrower in default can ask the sheriff court to suspend the enforcement of an eviction. The court can use its discretion to do so if either it considers you may be able to repay the arrears in a reasonable period of time, or the debtor and others staying at the home (such as your spouse or partner of either sex) need time to find other accommodation. You must make an application to court for this, and there are strict time limits and procedures for you to meet in order to stay the eviction for a time. The court does not automatically grant you the suspension, but looks into the whole circumstances of the case before deciding whether to or not.

Are there special powers for enforcing payment of council tax?

Yes. Councils don't need to go through a lengthy court procedure as do ordinary pursuers. If council tax is in arrears, the collecting authority can issue a notice, and add a percentage on to the unpaid amount as a penalty. In order to take enforcement action, the council can issue a summary warrant which allows it to arrest bank accounts and wages as if it had a court decree in its favour. If it has wrongly issued this warrant you can challenge it in court.

Chapter 18

Human Rights

A LAFFERTY

What areas of life do human rights laws cover?

Human rights in the United Kingdom are protected by the European Convention on Human Rights, commonly shortened to the ECHR. It includes:

- the right to life;
- prohibition of torture, inhuman or degrading treatment or punishment;
- prohibition of slavery and forced labour;
- right to liberty and security of person;
- right to a fair trial;
- no punishment if there is no law;
- right to respect for private and family life;
- freedom of thought, conscience and religion;
- freedom of expression;

- freedom of assembly and association;
- right to marry and found a family;
- no discrimination in respect of the Convention rights;
- right to protection of property, education and free elections; and
- abolition of the death penalty.

It is worth noting that some of these rights can be in conflict with each other: for example, if you have a religion that involves sacrificing virgins, this would clearly infringe on the right to life of the virgin.

How do you enforce a human right?

The United Kingdom has a duty to protect the rights and freedoms found in the European Convention on Human Rights. Included is a responsibility to ensure that domestic laws and procedures prevent harm or unfairness to individuals. A 'devolution issue' can be raised if it appears that an individual has been adversely affected by an act of the Scottish Executive or of the Scottish Parliament: for example, if a statute created by the Scottish Parliament contains provisions that are inconsistent with Convention rights. A devolution issue in criminal or civil proceedings may only be raised by a person who claims to be a victim of a violation of Convention rights. If a court or tribunal finds that a Convention right has been infringed, it can cancel or reduce the action, and in some cases award damages. Any person or group claiming to be a victim of a violation of one of their Convention rights by a member state can also sue their country in the European Court of Human Rights in Strasbourg, after exhausting all domestic legal avenues. The United Kingdom can then be made to change national law so as to comply with Convention articles. An example was the nine-year-old boy who suffered severe beatings with a garden cane at the hands of his stepfather. The stepfather was acquitted of assault in the English courts, using a defence of reasonable chastisement. The child petitioned that his rights to avoid inhuman and degrading treatment under the Convention had been breached, and that the United Kingdom should be held responsible. The boy was awarded damages to the sum of £10,000. It had traditionally in law been assumed that parents had the right to punish children corporally; this has now at least been very substantially reduced.

How do you know if your human rights are being infringed?

Consult your solicitor for advice or for referral to a sufficiently expert or specialised solicitor. The European Court of Human Rights has stressed that the European Convention on Human Rights is evolving and not fixed in stone. The basic framework of the Convention protects traditional, individual rights. Note that the Convention is the principal law; there are other more specific pieces of legislation from Europe.

Chapter 19

Lawmaking

Who makes our laws?

Our laws come from various sources, as below.

Legislation

The United Kingdom Parliament and the Scottish Parliament make laws called Acts or statutes, which are known as primary legislation. Often under those Acts, there is subordinate legislation such as regulations and orders which are more detailed rules to enforce the Acts or to allow a regulatory body created by the statute to operate. It is the Members of the relevant Parliament who technically pass the acts by voting, but in reality most new laws of this sort are created and put through by the government or executive of the day who have an inbuilt majority. Some matters, such as tax and defence, are United Kingdom-wide, and others, such as education and health, are the Scottish Parliament's responsibility. Remember we are also subject to legislation such as Directives from the European Union, and our Parliaments should not legislate in opposition to European law.

Judicial law

Our judges are bound by what is called precedent. This means that, if a judge or a court is deciding a point of law or a case, it is bound to follow a previous decision of a superior court on the same point if there is one. For example, the House of Lords may have decided a point about error in contracts. All future judges and courts lower down, such as the Court of Session and sheriff court, must decide similar cases in the same way. But if a point is then thought to be wrong, or circumstances have changed to make the point out of date, a court can decide the point differently; but to make the new point authoritative, the new decision must be by a court that is at least equal in rank to that which made the earlier one.

Common law

Some of our most basic law has been built up without being put in place by Act of Parliament. Usually this is the sort of thing that has been the subject of legal cases and problems for centuries: for example, theft or breach of the peace. With such matters, the courts accept that the law exists without it ever having been passed by Parliament, though often they have to interpret the law by reference to precedents in which the commission of common law offences has been considered.

How can an unfair law be challenged?

A citizen can try to get his or her MSP (Member of the Scottish Parliament) or MP (Member of Parliament) to get a new statute made in the appropriate Parliament, but this is a very tall order. Otherwise, under the Human Rights Act 1998, if an Act passed by the Scottish Parliament is considered to be unfair, an appeal against it can be taken to any court, as it breaches your human rights, which are now fundamental and enforceable.

We are part of the United Kingdom but Scotland has its own legal system; how does this work?

Before devolution, the Westminster Parliament made our legislative laws. Some Acts were for the whole of the United Kingdom, some for separate parts. Now that we have our own Parliament again, Edinburgh makes the new laws for Scotland, and London for England and Wales (Northern Ireland at the time of writing is still under direct rule due to political upheaval at the Assembly, but no doubt things will continue to change and develop there). There are, however, still many laws in place that straddle the north and south of the country. The easiest way to look at it is that Scotland makes and enforces its own laws on all areas of life except those which are retained matters (that is, not devolved to the Scottish Parliament). The main legal categories which are still British are: employment law, immigration, tax, state benefits, drugs and matters to do with the armed forces.

Chapter 20

Death

Can a person making a will disinherit family members?

I have tried to avoid using unnecessary technical legal language in this book, but some legal terms are essential when discussing rights in law. You can partly disinherit a spouse or children, but the law puts a limit on that. Spouses have the intestate succession right of *ius relicti* (husband) or *ius relictae* (wife) and children have the right of *legitim*. The law divides the estate of a deceased into three parts: the prior rights; the legal rights; and the free estate. After payment of debts and the removal of heritable property (houses and land), any money or assets that remain are divided up. If there are spouse and children, the spouse is entitled to one-third. If there are no children, the spouse gets a half. If there is a surviving spouse or parent, the children share a third among themselves; if no spouse, they share a half. The deceased cannot get out of this by trying to will everything to someone else.

If a married person dies without making a will, does their spouse not just get the lot?

It depends on the amount and make-up of the estate. The spouse has statutory prior rights to the following (but only if there is no will):

- not the house (if owned by the deceased) the survivor ordinarily lived in at the time of death (though if the deceased's interest in the home after deduction of an outstanding mortgage is worth more than £130,000 the survivor gets a cash award for that sum);

- the furniture and plenishings (an old fashioned legal word for furnishings) up to the value of £22,000;

- the first amount of money in the estate – up to £35,000 if there are surviving children, or £58,000 if there are none.

Only if there is estate left over after these entitlements are met do children come into reckoning for a share of the estate.

What is the order of priority in the family when someone dies without a will?

In the absence of a will to deal with the whole estate, the order, after paying debts and dealing with legal rights is:

(1)   children get equal shares (note that the eldest has no priority);
(2)   parents and brothers and sisters (half to each group);
(3)   brothers and sisters (if no parents);
(4)   parents (if no brothers and sisters);
(5)   spouse;
(6)   aunts and uncles;
(7)   grandparents; and
(8)   brothers and sisters of grandparents.

Note that each category takes the whole remaining estate. So if there are no children but there are brothers and sisters, there will be nothing left for the spouse.

What is the advantage or benefit in making a will?

Unless you have children or a spouse you want to disinherit as far as possible, a will is the only way of dividing up your estate as you wish. Without a will, no charity can benefit, nor can any friend. You cannot leave a memento or keepsake to a specific family member. Also, without a will your family will have a bigger and more expensive job to wind up your estate after your death.

What is the cost of making a will?

Some solicitors do wills for nothing, a sort of free gift, especially if you are consulting them about other business. Some will ask you to make a donation to charity. But if a fee is being charged, you can assume it will not likely be less than £25, and not more than £100, unless your estate or instructions are very complex. Your solicitor will generally retain the will in safe storage for you without charge, though it is your document and can be kept by you at home; however, this is risky as your home may be burgled or burn to the ground with you, and the will, in it.

What do you put in a will?

Three main things are needed to start with:

(1) Nomination of an executor, and also a reserve executor if the nominated one dies or is not able to take up the position after the death of the testator (perhaps as he is the testator's husband and dies with him in an accident). The executor's duties, such as payment of debts and funeral expenses, should be stated.

(2) A statement of any specific legacies the testator wishes to be paid, if any, to friends, family, churches, charities, or cat and dog homes. If a will is not made, no one except the closest family members will get any part of the estate.

(3) Division of the residue, which is what is left after the specific legacies, if any. The will may state that the estate is to be divided equally among the children. The question often needs to be asked: what if one of the children dies before the testator, leaving children of his own? Do those grandchildren inherit their parent's share, or is the share re-divided among the surviving children? The will must state what is to happen if any beneficiaries die.

There are other provisions that can be put in wills: for example, funeral arrangements, personal comments (good and bad), or powers for the executor to invest money for any under-age beneficiaries. Some younger testators state a wish in the will for any young children they leave behind to be cared for by a particular person. There is nothing wrong with doing this, but such a statement is not binding if a different person claims care of the children and goes to court to seek a parental rights order. The court will decide what is in the children's best interests at that point.

How can a will be challenged?

The very name 'will' presupposes the person making and signing it is doing so by their own deliberate and considered decision. Thus, if it can be proved that was not the case, then the will can be struck down. The main reasons why this happens are that the will is a forgery; that it was signed under some sort of duress; that the testator was incapable of truly understanding what he or she was doing when signing; that the testator was of weak will and easily led into making a will by unfair persuasion; or that there was undue influence by someone who took advantage of a position of trust (such as a solicitor who wrote the will to give himself a legacy in his own client's estate). If an aggrieved relative wants to challenge a will, he must do so in court, and prove by clear evidence (especially medical evidence in the case of an insanity case) that the will is not valid. This is a high hill to climb as supposition and suspicion are not enough. If the will was prepared by, or under the supervision of, a lawyer then it is likely that the lawyer will be able to say that he or she took care to check the willingness and understanding of the testator at the time.

What rights do spouses from second marriages, step-children and adopted children have?

Children retain the rights to their parents' estates no matter that a divorce has taken place (though the divorce ends a spouse's right to claim on the death of the ex-spouse). Step-children have no claim on the estate of step-parents; however, if a child is adopted, including by a step-parent, then he or she has a right of succession to that adoptive parent's estate, and no claim on the natural parent's estate.

What if two wills are found?

If two wills are found the later is presumed to overrule the earlier, so far as it is inconsistent with the earlier one. Indeed a well-drawn will should contain a clear clause stating that all previous wills are revoked.

What is an executor and what does he or she do?

The executor becomes the administrative officer for the estate. Whether he or she is a spouse or family member (it does not need to be an eldest child, or a son), a solicitor, or any other adult person, his duties commence on the death. He has the right to ingather the estate, correspond with banks and financial institutions and companies, and to apply to court for a confirmation order, to divide up the estate and settle debts, sell the deceased's property and generally do all that a will dictates (or, if no will, what the law requires). If the executor defaults or acts unlawfully, the beneficiaries can take him to court for what is called count, reckoning and payment to ensure that proper division of the estate takes place. If he retains the money due to beneficiaries, this may even amount to theft. The position of executor is unpaid unless the will says otherwise. The executor can be anybody nominated by the will, but, if there is no will, it should be a person who is entitled to a share of the estate by the law of intestate succession.

What is probate/confirmation?

Confirmation is the Scottish procedure to make the appointment of an executor more formal. Strictly speaking it is the order issued from the sheriff court in favour of the executor. It involves the sheriff court checking the inventory of estate and the information presented to court by the executor or solicitor on the deceased and the death, and granting a certificate that requires banks and any person or body holding the money belonging to the deceased to hand it over to the executor. Probate is the English equivalent.

Why won't the bank release the money of the deceased to the family automatically?

For convenience the bank can choose to settle the money due to the estate on the word of the executor, with appropriate ID and bank paperwork done. This will only happen if the amounts are small, and is more likely if there is a will in existence that makes clear provision where money is to go and appoints an executor whom the bank can recognise. If the bank chooses to insist on confirmation, however, it is entitled to do so. Banks are cautious in case there are perhaps other relatives with competing claims on the money; or if a person misrepresents facts or relationships to it; or if there is a subsequent will that the person claiming the money has not mentioned.

How can I avoid death duties/inheritance tax?

In 1986 inheritance tax replaced capital transfer tax, which in turn had replaced death duties in 1975. Inheritance tax is presently set at 40% of an estate worth over £255,000. Below £255,000 there is a total exemption from tax. There is also exemption when a spouse dies and there is a surviving spouse, whether or not there is a will. There are two main ways of legitimately avoiding tax. One is to give away enough of your estate during your life so that, when you die, you own less than the threshold figure. The downsides of this are twofold: firstly, it means you lose control over that part of your estate you have given away; secondly, the Inland Revenue looks back from the date of death, and any transfers of money or property a deceased made within that time (seven years), whether by gift or sale for below value, and includes within the estate the chargeable transfers made. The second way of avoiding tax is by creating a trust, which is a legitimate legal vehicle for the ownership of assets of different sorts. The trust is a different legal person from the maker of the trust or original owner, and hence does not die when the human individual dies. The disadvantages of this are that it can be complicated and sometimes expensive, and requires professional help in setting it up effectively and managing it on an ongoing basis.

How much does it cost to wind up an estate?

There is no fixed cost. If the estate is under £17,000 it is a small estate and the sheriff clerk of the local sheriff court can assist you in completing paperwork. If it is over that amount, then it depends on how extensive the estate is, and whether there is a will (if there is one, the costs are always less than for an intestate estate). If a deceased has a house and one bank account, the work to get a grant of confirmation will be small. If the deceased had, say, individual savings accounts (ISAs), shares, insurance, an overseas timeshare, a business and a dog, then there is considerably more correspondence for the solicitor to do. The cost will not be less than hundreds of pounds, and can go up to thousands.

How long is it before legacies are paid out?

Legacies should not be paid out earlier than six months after the death, but it may be longer if, for example, the executor is trying to track down distant family members, or has to get involved in lengthy correspondence about some parts of the estate, or if there is a dispute among family, or if the Department of Work and Pensions are investigating possible overpayment of benefits to the deceased during life, or there is income tax due by the deceased, or to him. It is a matter for the executor as to how and when to finalise the estate. If the beneficiaries think it is taking far too long, they are entitled to go to court for an order to force settlement.

What happens if a long-lost relative turns up after winding up?

A relative or named beneficiary that was known about is entitled to insist on payment or receipt of a legacy or share of residue up to 20 years after the death, after which the right prescribes, that is, it is lost. He can sue the executor for payment.

What is a living will, and is it legal?

A living will is a statement of intent. In the event that the testator will in the future be badly injured or fall terminally ill, the instruction is that there is to be no resuscitation or life-preserving medical treatment. Some people even go further, but euthanasia is still a crime in this country. The will does not have the force of law, and is no more than an expression of a wish. It can guide relatives and medical staff, but cannot bind them to act or refrain from acting as they see fit.

Who has to register a death and when?

Every death must be registered in the Register of Deaths for the appropriate district within eight days from the date of death, or from the date of finding of the body. Certain people have a legal duty to go to the registry office and give information to the best of their knowledge, as well as to sign the Register in the Registrar's presence. Those people are:

- any relative of the deceased;
- any person present at the death;
- the deceased's executor or other legal representative;
- the occupier, at the time of death, of the premises where the death took place; or
- if none of the foregoing apply, any other person having knowledge of the particulars to be registered.

What happens if a death is suspicious?

In every death, a doctor provides a certificate of cause of death, to the best of his knowledge. A doctor, the police or a registrar may refer a suspicious death to the Procurator Fiscal, who may interview relatives and other witnesses, or ask the police to assist, call for a further medical report or order a post-mortem. If the death gives rise to serious public concern, a fatal accident inquiry may be arranged. This is held in the sheriff court. When the Procurator Fiscal's investigations are completed, the Registrar-General is notified of the findings. Note that if, as a consequence of investigations, the culprit is found to be someone who would benefit or inherit from the estate of the deceased, they are barred from such inheritance.

Chapter 21

Legal Costs and Legal Aid

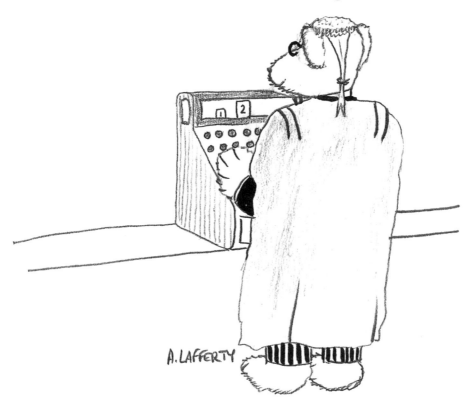

A. LAFFERTY

How can I find out how much a solicitor is going to charge me?

Solicitors have a scale of charges based on an approved Law Society of Scotland rate known as the unit. The units cover time spent, and paperwork produced. All work can be broken down into numbers of units. The Law Society of Scotland issues a charge per unit, and standard fees for private work are charged according to this. At the moment the unit is £11.30 and there are ten units in one hour, and each page of a letter or document produced is one unit. Unfortunately, this equation will not help most clients in knowing what their overall fees will be. There are so many variables and so many different types of business that no one can tell how much work will be necessary in, for example, a civil or divorce case, or when it will be completed. What appears to be a routine case may bring in unforeseen complexities. However, your solicitor will be able, and is obliged, to give you an estimate of fees at the outset, and certainly to outline the basis of charging. There is nothing to stop you negotiating a different fee or fixed cost arrangement if the solicitor is willing. For conveyancing many solicitors have a set charge per transaction. You are entitled to a statement of fees and outlays (for example, stamp duty land tax, registration dues, searches or mining reports) at the outset of a conveyancing transaction.

Will I have to pay my solicitor in advance?

It is up to you and your solicitor to agree the method and time of payment. You are best to do this before the work has started. A solicitor is not obliged to carry out work if payment is outstanding unless it was agreed beforehand that payment would be on conclusion. You can enter a written fee agreement with the solicitor.

What if I am unhappy about fees or think I have been overcharged?

Every solicitor must be able to justify his fees. If a client is not satisfied, then he can have the account taxed, that is, referred to the auditor of the local sheriff court, who can state what the fee should be. If overcharging happens, it can be cancelled back to the correct amount. However, if the fee has actually been properly charged, it will be the client who pays the cost of the auditor, as well as paying the fee. If there has been fraudulent or oppressive conduct by the solicitor, the client can make a complaint to the Law Society of Scotland. The lawyer can be reprimanded, fined, made to pay back some or all of the fee, or even suspended or struck off from practice in the most serious cases.

Is legal aid available for civil court cases?

Legal aid is available, subject to rules on your means and the merits of your case, for pursuing or defending actions in the civil courts. This includes divorces, family cases, compensation actions, contract disputes and employment tribunal cases. For initial work by a solicitor in the office, such as advising you, taking statements, corresponding with opposing solicitors and work preparatory to going to court, the legal aid is known as Advice and Assistance. When going to court, you are granted either civil or criminal legal aid.

Can I get a first free interview with a solicitor ?

Only if he or she agrees or has this as a firm policy. The Yellow Pages often carries adverts from lawyers who offer this. All you need to do is ask the solicitor in advance of any consultation to find out.

Do all solicitors work on legal aid, and do you get a better service paying privately?

No and no. There is no pecking order that I am aware of. Many extremely expert and specialist solicitors act under legal aid. Some only do legal aid work and, although not all solicitors are of equal expertise in all matters, all solicitors are under a duty to carry out clients' work in the best interests of those clients. This includes making the client aware that legal aid is available or that they may qualify for it, rather than just automatically charging a higher private rate.

How do I know if I qualify for legal aid?

Your solicitor is able to judge both from experience and a rough calculation based on information taken from you as to your likely eligibility. There are certain 'passport' benefits which allow you legal aid eligibility on income automatically. The solicitor will assist you to complete the application and send it in with the necessary documentation to the Scottish Legal Aid Board. Remember, even if you qualify financially, you still have to convince the Board that you have a *probable cause*, that is, a winnable or arguable case.

How much in the way of assets or income puts me over the limit for legal aid?

Every person's case and circumstances are different, but, for Advice and Assistance, any legal aid solicitor can assess you on the spot. For civil or criminal legal aid, the Scottish Legal Aid Board assesses you, and either grants or refuses legal aid after this. You can re-apply if your financial circumstances change.

What does legal aid cover?

Once legal aid is granted, it covers the fees for advice, drawing and revising legal pleadings, court representation by lawyers, letters and calls made by your solicitor on your behalf, and outlays, which are costs for expert witnesses, doctors or other specialists. The solicitor may need to ask the Scottish Legal Aid Board for specific sanction or permission to pay for specialist witnesses or documents needed to help fight the case as it goes along.

Does it cover all the costs or do I have to pay something?

In criminal legal aid, if you are granted a certificate, you have nothing to pay. In civil legal aid and Advice and Assistance, you may be required to pay a contribution towards the costs. For civil legal aid, that can be from tens of pounds to over a thousand, payable by instalments. If you are on certain 'passport' benefits, you automatically are excluded from paying a contribution.

Is there a clawback of legal aid from any award I get?

If you achieve a payment in a case either by way of court order or a settlement out of court after legal aid is in place, the Scottish Legal Aid Board has the first call on the money recovered, which usually is paid in the first place to your solicitor on your behalf. Your solicitor must hold back enough to cover your legal aid fees and lodge this with the Board until his account has been assessed and he is to be paid his fees. The balance will be paid to you. If you have been awarded expenses (costs) by the court, then these will be set against your fees to reduce any amount due by you, but usually court-awarded (judicial) expenses do not cover everything, and not preliminary work done before the action was raised. In divorce cases the first £4,200 awarded to a successful spouse is not subject to the clawback.

Once legal aid is in place is it permanent?

Legal aid stays in place until the end of a case or earlier termination. Legal aid can be stopped if your circumstances change and you suddenly no longer qualify: for example, if you have started a highly paid job. It can also be cancelled if you don't pay the allotted contribution or break the rules. Anyone on legal aid must tell the Scottish Legal Aid Board if they have had a change of circumstances; failure to do so can cause the legal aid to be withdrawn and can also be a criminal offence. Note that legal aid for court work may be granted conditionally, to be reviewed when the case reaches a certain point.

Chapter 22

Miscellaneous

Do contracts need to be in writing?

The general rule is that writing is not required for the creation of a valid contract in Scots law (there is a terrible old legal joke about a verbal contract not being worth the paper it is written on). It is sufficient that both people have the intention to create legal relations; however, there are some exceptions to this rule. Any transactions involving land must be in writing in order to constitute a legally valid contract. There must be written agreement by both parties. In a contract for the sale of land this would be contained in the missives. Writing is also required in some cases in order to clarify the position of the more vulnerable party. For example, a contract of employment should be in written form so that the employee is aware of the terms and conditions of his employment.

How can a lawyer defend someone when he knows they are guilty?

A lawyer generally does not know if his or her client is guilty unless the client tells him. Note that even guilty persons are entitled to legal representation as far as is appropriate in law and ethics. If the accused does admit guilt, then the lawyer advises a plea of guilty. If the client does not take that advice, then the lawyer is very restricted in what he can do to defend. He cannot, for example, cross-examine prosecution witnesses to accuse them of lying if he is aware they are telling the truth. Indeed, the lawyer will probably feel unable to represent this accused at all if he pleads not guilty, and will resign from the case. The more common situation is that of an accused person saying to his lawyer that he did not do it, and, although there is strong evidence against him, that he is not guilty. Here the lawyer may not judge the client, or put his own prejudices or suspicions ahead of his duty to the client; that duty is to represent the client to the best of his ability. It is a fundamental duty, and is part of our civilised system of justice. If someone is being prosecuted by the state, there are two factors which are crucial. One is that the prosecutor is a professional lawyer and it would be unfair if the accused did not have the right to equality of arms. The second is that every accused is innocent until proved guilty. We do not have trial by tabloid, thank goodness.

What if I want to complain about my solicitor?

You should firstly raise any question with the solicitor him or herself. If you are still unhappy you should write a formal letter of complaint to the firm's senior partner or complaints partner. If the firm cannot resolve matters to your satisfaction, you can write a letter of complaint to the Law Society of Scotland, who will investigate it. The Law Society of Scotland will either decide that the complaint is unfounded, or will accept it and make an order of one sort or another. It may order the solicitor to refund part or all of your fee or to carry out some other action. If there is serious enough misconduct by the solicitor, the Society may refer the case against the lawyer for prosecution at the Scottish Solicitors Discipline Tribunal. Although the Scottish Solicitors Discipline Tribunal has some solicitors on it as well as lay persons, it is independent of the Society and has various powers, including the power to strike a solicitor off the roll of solicitors. The solicitor is entitled to be represented at hearings of the Tribunal. The Tribunal can suspend a solicitor; fine him; reduce him to acting as an assistant to other solicitors; or reprimand him.

Can I sue someone who attacks my character for defamation/slander/libel?

Attacks on personal or professional honesty or integrity are called defamation. If written, for example, in a newspaper or a letter, it is libel. If spoken, then it is known as slander. If a statement is false then the victim can claim financial damages. These are calculated on the basis of how serious and damaging the attack was. The defences to an accusation of defamation include *veritas* (the truth), fair comment and privilege. Privilege can be claimed by a person making a defamatory remark when it is made within a court case or Parliament. Also, if a matter of public importance is discussed and inaccuracies occur, then, if there is no malice intended, there may be no right to action. Be warned, however, that legal aid is *not* available for defamation actions. There is a legal saying that often applies to defamation cases: 'strong principles ruined more folk than strong drink ever did'.

How do I maintain copyright on something I have written or created?

There is no copyright on ideas, just the expression of them. You should therefore make printed or written copies of any songs, stories, plans, computer programs, TV formats, game shows and do the following: put at least one in a sealed envelope, and send it by recorded delivery to yourself or to someone like a solicitor. That will be carefully stored, so that if someone uses your idea, you can prove that you dated it and the date on which it was written. Copyright is not registered, but copyright in a work ends at least 50 years after the creator's death. In contrast, patents on inventions are granted and registered by the Patent Office and are for a limited period. Copyright and patent law are very contentious and complex, but this is a start at least.

What are my responsibilities for any animal I own?

If you have failed to control, supervise or pen an animal and it causes damage or bites someone, you may be liable in damages to the victim. If they caused or contributed to the incident by leaving a gate open or baiting a dog then blame may fall on them. If your dog has attacked someone you can be prosecuted in the criminal courts and in extreme cases the dog may be destroyed. If you neglect or are cruel to animals you own, you can be prosecuted, and if convicted, disqualified from owning animals in the future.

Do we have a law of privacy?

Not really; however, in some relationships there is either an explicit or implied duty of confidentiality. An example is the relationship between employer and employee, which can extend beyond the end of the employment relationship, so that trade secrets and commercially sensitive information cannot legally be made public or passed on to strangers or competitors. There is, however, no inherent duty to keep secrets or to refrain from telling stories about people or events that you know about, even if this is embarrassing to those who are spoken of. The only remedy a victim of gossip or scandal has is to sue if the information is not correct and is damaging. Media organisations are bound by codes of practice not to go beyond certain limits in reporting on people's private lives, particularly in stories involving children, but there are few legal constraints; an exception is where there is a court order to prevent publication of certain information which is part of a court case.

Can I enforce a gambling debt? What if I am in a lottery syndicate and we win?

The law specifically denies anyone owed a gambling debt or bet the right to sue in the civil courts. But if there are winnings, and there is a prior agreement to share them, as in a lottery syndicate, then a member who has not been paid can sue the others for payment under breach of contract. If the person in the syndicate who puts the stake on keeps the money, he or she is in breach of a contract of agency on behalf of the others and can be sued for payment.

Can I make a citizen's arrest? What if someone breaks into my house?

The police are not the only people with the power to make an arrest as the law still recognises a citizen's arrest, though it is so rare as to be exceptional, and usually leads to tabloid newspaper stories about have-a-go-heroes or umbrella-wielding grannies. As a member of the public you may arrest someone who is committing an arrestable offence, such as theft or assault, or where you reasonably suspect that such an offence has been committed. You can even use reasonable force in doing so. However, unless you are very careful, you could be accused of committing an assault, especially if you use excessive force. If someone is in your house unlawfully, you should be even more careful. The courts have convicted householders of assault or even murder when confrontations with burglars have gone too far. You may not set traps or urge dogs to attack intruders. Defence is only lawful self-defence if you are in actual unavoidable danger when you hit out, or at least reasonable anticipation of this, or acting in the necessary defence of another.

What constitutes self-defence?

If you are attacked, or someone with you is attacked, you have the right to defend yourself physically. You can do so only if there is no non-violent alternative, and, if the chance to escape or get help from police is available, you must try those options. You can only respond in proportion to the assault. If someone tries to punch you, you cannot then draw a knife on them. Indeed, not only would you be committing an assault, you would be guilty of the offence of either carrying a knife or being in possession of an offensive weapon. There is no defence of 'square-go', that is, if you are in an agreed fight, or return someone's initial blow to even things up. This would amount to a criminal assault by you (the other person of course having committed an assault first). Note that while the courts will possibly be sympathetic up to a point if you are provoked, you are still committing a crime when lashing out in response to provocation.

Do we have freedom of information in Scotland?

The Freedom of Information (Scotland) Act 2002 enables any person to obtain recorded information from Scottish public authorities, including the Scottish Executive and its agencies; the Scottish Parliament; local authorities; the National Health Service for Scotland; universities and colleges; and the police. From 2005 any person who makes a request for information must be provided with it, subject to certain conditions. The Act places an obligation on all Scottish public authorities to adopt and maintain a 'publication scheme'. This scheme sets out the categories of information the authority publishes, the manner in which it is published, and details of any charges for receiving the information. Access must be allowed to the provision, cost and standard of an authority's service; factual information or decision-making; and the reasons for decisions made by it. There will be exemptions, such as for information relating to national security and defence, specific police investigations and the formulation or development of government policy. If a public authority decides not to release information, as it considers it exempt, it must give reasons for its decision. This 'refusal notice' will allow the applicant to ask the authority to review their decision, and then, if the information has still been withheld, to seek a determination from the Scottish Information Commissioner.

How does data protection legislation work?

The law now covers personal data in both electronic form and manual form, such as files; if held in a structured filing system personal data must be obtained fairly and lawfully. It must be kept accurate and up to date and shall not be kept for longer than is necessary. The person whose data is being obtained or stored should be informed of who the data controller and his representative is; the reasons for which the data is intended to be used; and to whom the data will be disclosed. Personal data processing may only take place if specific conditions have been met: these include you having given consent or the processing being necessary for the legitimate interests of the data controller. Additional conditions must be satisfied for the processing of sensitive personal data, concerning ethnic origin, political persuasion and union involvement, religion, health, sexuality or criminal background.

Your individual rights are to:

- make a subject access request as you are entitled to be supplied with a copy of all data held;

- require the data controller to ensure that no significant decisions that affect you are based solely upon an automated decision-taking process;

- prevent processing likely to cause damage or distress;

- prevent processing for the purposes of direct marketing;

- get compensation if you are damaged by any breach of the Act by the data controller;
- have inaccurate data rectified, or destroyed; and
- request the Information Commissioner to make an assessment as to whether your rights have been breached.

What are the laws on immigration?

Some of the issues that arise for people coming to the United Kingdom include how long they can stay; whether they can work while they are here; whether relatives can come to the United Kingdom to join them; whether they can use the National Health Service or claim benefits. Britain is a single unit for this area of law, so Scotland does not have separate rules. British citizenship can be relevant, as the regulations about who can come in to the country, for what purpose and with whom depend on the status of the persons involved. Immigration issues can be very complex and subject to change. Within the legal profession only specialised solicitors can give the appropriate up-to-date advice. The Law Society of Scotland can provide reference to such solicitors: see the useful contacts section.

Glossary

Abatement — bring to a stop a legal nuisance.

Abduction — the removal of a person by means of force without legal excuse or the person's consent.

Absolvitor — a final decree in a civil case in favour of the defender which prevents the pursuer from trying to take the case to court again.

Aliment — maintenance that can be claimed by a spouse or child who has a financial need. Interim aliment is available for urgent need.

Acquit — to find the accused in a criminal trial not guilty or not proven.

Arrestment — where the court orders the freezing of earnings, bank accounts, or other assets so they cannot be used until a debt is paid.

Attachment — a warrant of attachment can be granted to enable an officer of the court to seize and sell certain assets of a debtor.

Balance of probabilities — the standard of proof needed in civil cases. The standard for criminal law is beyond a reasonable doubt, which is a higher one.

Bankruptcy — a state which a person can opt for or can be ordered into if his debts are such that he cannot pay them.

Beneficiary — someone receiving a benefit from a will or other such deed.

Breach — occurs when a term of an order or contract is violated.

Breach of the peace — currently defined as 'conduct which does present as genuinely alarming and disturbing, in its context, to any reasonable person'.

Charge — there are two types. In criminal law it is the wording of the accusation laid at an accused person. In civil law it is the commencement of diligence (enforcement) of a court order, and is drawn up and served by a sheriff officer on the unsuccessful party.

Citation — citing witnesses has the effect of a court order forcing them to appear at court. They can be punished and held in contempt of court if they fail to appear.

Civil law — involves the rights and duties in legal relationships between any combination of private citizens, corporate and public bodies.

Clawback — deduction of a portion of a civil award or settlement for legal aid or benefits reasons.

Common law — law that does not come from statutes made by Parliament, but is laid down in the decisions of judges in cases that come before them.

Compensation — awards made in cases for injury to a party, whether physical or other.

Confirmation — the Scottish procedure of the sheriff court formally appointing an executor over the estate of a deceased person.

Constructive dismissal — where an employer is in breach of contract and the employee feels that he has been forced into resigning as a result. It is treated as a dismissal by the employer for tribunal purposes.

Contact order (previously access) — an order governing contact (that is visitation, care and holidays) by a person with a child they are not living with.

Contributory negligence — where a person contributed to an accident or claim event through their own actions. Such a finding may reduce an award, to nil in some cases.

Conveyancing — the process of sale and purchase of land and buildings.

Copyright — a property right in original artistic and other works.

Court order — an order by the court to do or not do something that can be enforced.

Curator ad litem — a solicitor who is appointed to look after the interests of the child in court.

Damages — an amount of money awarded as compensation for loss, injury or damage that a person has suffered as a result of an act or omission of someone else.

Decree — the final order of court.

Devolution — the transfer of law-making powers from the United Kingdom to parliaments or assemblies of Northern Ireland, Scotland and Wales. This happened in 1999 for the Scottish Parliament.

Diligence — the enforcement of court decrees by sheriff officers and messengers-at-arms.

Discrimination — involves treating someone unfairly or differently because of their sex, sexual orientation, marital status, pregnancy, religion, race or disability.

Estate — a person's property, assets and debts left on their death.

Executor — a person nominated by a testator to wind up his estate on death.

Guardian — can be appointed to look after the physical welfare and/or the financial affairs of a child or of an incapacitated adult.

Heritable property — generally houses and land.

Inhibition — an order by the Court of Session that prevents the owner from disposing of property or burdening it to defeat a financial claim by another party pursuing him.

Interdict — an order by the court preventing someone from starting or carrying on an activity (the English equivalent is an injunction).

Interlocutor — an official document containing the order or judgment of the court in a civil action.

Intestate — describes the estate of a person who dies without leaving a will.

Joint and several — an obligation on more than one person that can be collected from one of them or from all of them together.

Judicial review — a civil case in which the government or a public body is sued for defeating a person's legal rights by their actions.

Jurisdiction — the area of law or the region that falls within the authority of a court or public body.

Land certificate — the document issued by the Land Register of Scotland that proves ownership of land.

Land Register of Scotland — the map-based register of all Land Certificates that is over time replacing the old Sasine recording of deeds.

Lease — a document stating the rights and duties of the parties to a tenancy.

Legacy — money or moveable property left in a will to a beneficiary.

Legal aid — provides legal assistance for individuals who are unable to afford representation or may otherwise be unable to afford access to the legal system.

Legislation — laws that are passed by Parliament, sometimes called primary legislation. Orders, rules and regulations are subordinate legislation.

Liable — subject to a legal obligation.

Loss of earnings — a type of damages to compensate for money that would have been earned if an injured person had been able to stay at work.

Loss of society — a type of damages to attempt to compensate for the loss of the company of a close family member whose (mainly) parent, child or spouse has been killed in an accident.

Loss of support — a type of damages to support the family where the person who died in an accident previously provided the means of support.

Matrimonial property — property that is owned by both parties that may be divided on separation or divorce.

Minute of agreement — a written contract of agreed terms which is signed, registered and enforceable.

Minute of tender — a written statement from one of the parties of what that they are prepared to pay in a set sum in damages.

Missives — a written contract that is concluded between the seller and purchaser of land or buildings by way of exchanged letters.

Moveable property — any property that is not heritable property.

Nuisance — legal nuisance arises from activities that are generally incompatible with peaceful coexistence. The behaviour must be considered unreasonable, and cause actual harm, inconvenience or discomfort.

Ombudsman — an official who is appointed to investigate complaints of citizens in different areas.

Ordinary cause — in the sheriff court for civil cases for sums greater than £1,500 or for non-financial matters.

Patent — a right granted for inventions for a specified period through registration with the Patent Office.

Poind — (pronounced *pinned*) an older form of diligence used to impound a debtors property before a warrant sale is undertaken.

Precedent — judges and courts are bound to follow the decisions of superior courts where they have decided on the same point of law as in the case before them.

Probate — English court order for winding up a deceased person's estate. Often mistakenly asked by banks and insurance companies for Scottish estates. (See also confirmation).

Proof — a first hearing in a civil court before a judge which hears evidence and decides on matters of fact.

Provocation — words or actions which have the effect of stirring someone into committing a violent crime.

Qualified acceptance — in a conveyancing transaction where there is acceptance with some condition placed on it.

Reasonable doubt — the standard of proof in criminal cases. The prosecution must prove their case beyond the point where there can be any doubt that is reasonable that the defendant committed the act accused of.

Redundancy — where an employee's job no longer exists due to such circumstances as reorganisation or automation of the workplace.

Residence (previously custody) — where a child lives with a parent or other adult.

Re-engagement — being re-employed by the same employer in a different job from the one that you were dismissed from.

Reinstatement — being put back into the job that you were dismissed from or one similar.

Sasine — the Sasine recording of deeds has its roots in the feudal system of the middle ages, it is now being replaced by the Land Register of Scotland.

Separation date — when spouses start living separately or, if staying in the same house due to children or financial necessity, living separate lives.

Sequestration — the process of going into bankruptcy where the bankrupt's property is put into the hands of an appointed trustee.

Settlement — when a case is settled between the parties before the court decides the case.

Small claim — in the sheriff court for civil cases involving sums up to £750.

Solatium — a type of damages for pain and suffering.

Statute — an Act that is passed by Parliament.

Summary cause — in the sheriff court for civil matters involving sums between £750 and £1,500.

Testator — a person who dies with a valid will for the disposal of his estate.

Time bar — a period of time after an incident which prevents a claim for compensation being pursued.

Title deeds — are drawn up when land or buildings are sold and registered with the Land Register of Scotland.

Trespass — the temporary intrusion into the property of another without the permission of the owner or lawful occupier.

Unjustified enrichment — when one person has been financially advantaged at another's expense without a lawful excuse.

Vicarious liability — where someone is responsible for the actions or omission of others due to their relationship or position, most often for employees and agents.

Void — not valid.

Warrant — the court's authority to enforce what is stated in an order. There are different types of warrant in civil and criminal cases.

Warranty — a purchased warranty is a contract, and both parties (buyer and seller) are bound by the precise terms of it. A warranty can only enhance, not limit, your statutory consumer rights.

Will — a signed document made by a testator directing what is to happen to his estate after his death. Includes the appointment of an executor, specific legacies, and division of the residue of the estate.

Useful Contacts

Austin Lafferty Solicitors
Head Office Mercantile Chambers
53 Bothwell Street
Glasgow G2 6TS
tel 0141 204 2522
fax 0141 204 2521
email alafferty@laffertylaw.com

Accountant in Bankruptcy
George House
126 George Street
Edinburgh EH2 4HH
tel 0131 473 4600
helpline 0845 762 6171
email info@aib.gov.uk
website www.aib.gov.uk

Advocates, Faculty of
Advocates Library
Parliament House
Edinburgh EH1 1RF
tel 0131 226 5071
website www.advocates.org.uk

Banking Code Standards Board
33 St James's Square
London SW1Y 4JS
tel 0207 661 9694
website
www.bankingcode.org.uk

British Standards Institution
389 Chiswick High Road
London W4 4AL
tel 0208 996 9000
email cservices@bsi-global.com
website www.bsi.org.uk

Child Support Agency
Parklands
Callendar Business Park
Callendar Road
Falkirk FK1 1XT
tel 08456 090042
(emailing facility available within
the website)
website www.csa.org.uk

Citizens Advice Bureau
Spectrum House
2 Powderhall Road
Edinburgh EH7 4GB
tel 0131 550 1000
email info@cas.org.uk
website www.cas.org.uk

Companies House
(UK registry of companies)
Companies House
37 Castle Terrace
Edinburgh EH1 2EB
tel 0870 33 33 636
email enquiries@companies-
house.gov.uk
website
www.companieshouse.gov.uk

**Consumer Credit Counselling
Service**
Wade House
Merrion Centre
Leeds LS2 8NG
tel 0800 138 1111
email contactus@cccs.co.uk
website www.cccssecure.co.uk

**Criminal Injuries Compensation
Authority**
Tay House
330 Bath Street
Glasgow G2 4LN
tel 0800 358 3601
website www.cica.gov.uk

Disability Rights Commission
DRC Helpline
Freepost
MID 02164
Stratford Upon Avon CV37 9BR
helpline 08457 622 633
textphone 08457 622 644
email enquiry@drc-gb.org
website www.drc-gb.org

Edinburgh Customer Service Centre
Erskine House
68 Queen Street
Edinburgh EH2 4NF
tel 0845 607 0161
email
customer.services@ros.gov.uk

Fair Trading, Director General of
OFT, Fleetbank House
2–6 Salisbury Square
London EC4Y 8JX
tel 08457 22 44 99
email enquiries@oft.gsi.gov.uk
website www.oft.gov.uk

Financial Services Authority
25 The North Colonnade
Canary Wharf
London E14 5HS
tel 0845 606 1234
email consumerhelp@fsa.gov.uk
website www.fsa.gov.uk

Financial Services Compensation Scheme
7th floor Lloyds Chambers
Portsoken Street
London E1 8BN
tel 0207 892 7300
email enquiries@fscs.org.uk
website www.fscs.org.uk

Financial Services Ombudsman
Considers complaints about a wide range of issues from insurance and mortgages to pensions and investments.
South Quay Plaza
183 Marsh Wall
London E14 9SR
tel 0845 080 1800
email complaint.info@financial-ombudsman.org.uk
website www.financial-ombudsman.org.uk

General Register Office
Change of Name Unit
New Register House
Edinburgh EH1 3YT
tel 0131 314 4404
fax 0131 314 4400
email namechange@gro-scotland.gov.uk
website
www.gro-scotland.gov.uk

Government Information Service
website www.open.gov.uk

Health and Safety Executive
Caerphilly Business Park
Caerphilly CF83 3GG
tel 08701 545500
email hseinformationservices@natbrit.com
website www.hse.gov.uk

Inland Revenue
Details of how to contact your local office can be found on the website.
website
www.inlandrevenue.gov.uk

Law Society of England and Wales
The Law Society's Hall
113 Chancery Lane
London WC2A 1PL
tel 0207 242 1222
email
info.services@lawsociety.org.uk
website www.lawsociety.org.uk

Law Society of Scotland
26 Drumsheugh Gardens
Edinburgh EH3 7YR
tel 0131 226 7411
email lawscot@lawscot.org.uk
website www.lawscot.org.uk

Mortgage Code Compliance Board
University Court
Stafford ST18 0GN
tel 01785 218200
email
enquiries@mortgagecode.org.uk
website
www.mortgagecode.org.uk

National Debtline
The Arch
48–52 Floodgate Street
Birmingham B5 5SL
tel 0808 808 4000
website
www.nationaldebtline.co.uk

Public Guardian, Office of the
Hadrian House
Callendar Business Park
Callendar Road FK1 1XR
tel 01324 678 300
email opg@scotcourts.gov.uk
website www.publicguardian-scotland.gov.uk

Registers of Scotland
Glasgow Customer Service Centre
9 George Square
Glasgow G2 1DY
tel 0845 607 0164 or
0141 306 4425
email
customer.services@ros.gov.uk
website www.ros.gov.uk

Royal Institution of Chartered Surveyors in Scotland
RICS Scotland
9 Manor Place
Edinburgh EH3 7DN
tel 0131 225 7078
email webenquiries@rics.org.uk
website www.rics-scotland.org.uk

Scottish Courts Administration
Scottish Court Service
Hayweight House
23 Lauriston Street
Edinburgh EH3 9DQ
tel 0131 229 9200
website www.scotcourts.gov.uk

Scottish Criminal Cases Review Commission
Portland House
5th Floor
17 Renfield Street
Glasgow G2 5AH
tel 0141 270 7030
fax 0141 270 7040/7023
email info@sccrc.org.uk

Scottish Environment Protection Agency
SEPA Corporate Office
Erskine Court
Castle Business Park
Stirling FK9 4TR
tel 01786 457700
Pollution hotline 0800 80 70 60
Flooding hotline 0845 988 1188
website www.sepa.org.uk

Scottish Executive
Addresses for individual
departments can be found on the
website.
tel Edinburgh 0131 556 8400
tel Glasgow 0141 248 2855
email ceu@scotland.gov.uk
website www.scotland.gov.uk

Scottish Information Commissioner
Kinburn Castle
Doubledykes Road
St Andrews, Fife KY16 9DS
tel 01334 464 610
fax 01334 464 611
email enquiries@
itspublicknowledge.info

Scottish Legal Aid Board
44 Drumsheugh Gardens
Edinburgh EH3 7SW
tel 0131 226 7061
email general@slab.org.uk
website www.slab.org.uk

Scottish Legal Services Ombudsman
17 Waterloo Place
Edinburgh EH1 3DL
tel 0131 556 9123
email ombudsman@slso.org.uk

Scottish Parliament
Edinburgh EH99 1SP
tel 0131 348 5000 or
0845 278 1999
email
sp.info@scottish.parliament.uk
website
www.scottish.parliament.uk

Scottish Public Services Ombudsman
4 Melville Street
Edinburgh EH3 7NS
tel 0870 011 5378
email enquiries@
scottishombudsman.org.uk
website
www.scottishombudsman.org.uk

Scottish Trades Union Congress
333 Woodlands Road
Glasgow G3 6NG
tel 0141 337 8100
email info@stuc.org.uk
website www.stuc.org.uk

Trading Standards
Details of how to contact your
local office are available from the
website.
website
www.tradingstandards.gov.uk

United Kingdom Patent Office
Concept House
Cardiff Road
Newport
South Wales NP10 8QQ
tel 0845 9500 505
email enquiries@patent.gov.uk
website www.patent.gov.uk

Victim Support Scotland
15/23 Hardwell Close
Edinburgh EH8 9RX
tel 0131 668 4486
email info@
victimsupportsco.demon.co.uk
website www.
victimsupportsco.demon.co.uk

Work and Pensions, Department of
Details of the various helplines are
available on the website.
website www.dwp.gov.uk

Index